Behavioral Insights for Development

DIRECTIONS IN DEVELOPMENT
Countries and Regions

Behavioral Insights for Development

Cases from Central America

Oscar Calvo-González and Laura Zoratto, Editors

Contents

Foreword

In its efforts to support countries in Central America, the World Bank is committed to bringing development solutions that tap into all available instruments for policy makers in a variety of disciplines, including sociology, psychology, and neuroscience. An emerging field of knowledge known as behavioral science helps explain why individuals make certain decisions in different areas of their lives, from savings and investment to energy consumption and health, among others. It also explains how collective behaviors develop and become ingrained in a society. Crucially, it can help design better programs and improve public service delivery.

The United Kingdom was the first country in which the government introduced the use of behavioral science for the design and delivery of its public policies and programs. Following its success, other countries such as Australia, Canada, and the United States have also begun to employ behavioral insights in refining their programs. Although the new approach seemed promising, it still needed to be tested in a development context.

This publication summarizes five cases in which the World Bank, in collaboration with governments and partners, has explored how to put this approach into practice in Central America. These experiences vary from efforts to elicit individual behavior change (such as encouraging water conservation in Costa Rica and increasing tax compliance in Guatemala) to complex social ones (such as enhancing child development in Nicaragua and better understanding the perceptions of subsidy reform in El Salvador).

The experiences from Central America shared in this volume draw from the experiences of a rapidly growing set of countries that are leveraging behavioral insights for development. With more than 80 behaviorally informed projects across 50 countries, the World Bank has established a Mind, Behavior, and Development (eMBeD) Unit within the Poverty and Equity Global Practice to mainstream and scale up behavioral science in public policies and programs. The eMBeD unit resulted from the publication of *World Development Report 2015: Mind, Society, and Behavior*, which showed how behavioral insights can benefit development initiatives. Central America presents multiple opportunities where behavioral insights can continue to enhance development, from encouraging saving behavior to reducing gender-based violence.

As development practitioners, we need to use all available resources and tools at hand to fight global poverty and increase equity. The examples from Central America reflected in this volume demonstrate how a more nuanced understanding of the drivers of human behavior can help improve project design and lead to better outcomes.

J. Humberto López
*Director for Strategy and Operations for Latin America and
the Caribbean and former Country Director for Central America
The World Bank Group*

Acknowledgments

We would like to acknowledge the unwavering support of many individuals over the past three years, during which the activities described in this book took place. In particular, the team would like to thank the World Bank's country directors of the Central America Country Management Unit—Humberto López and, until 2014, Felipe Jaramillo—for their guidance and support. Other members of the Central America team, including Oscar Avalle, Desiree González, Andrea Kucey, Àngels Masó, Camille Nuamah, Maryanne Sharp, Jovana Stojanovic, and Fabrizio Zarcone were instrumental in launching this work program. We are also grateful for the guidance provided by Arturo Herrera. Courtney Irvin provided valuable support to submit this book for publication.

The book draws on background papers prepared by staff from the World Bank's Global Practices for Governance, Poverty and Equity, Macroeconomics and Fiscal Management, and Environment and Natural Resources. María González de Asís, Marcelo Buitron, and Saugato Datta organized the brainstorming on behavioral insights at the 2013 Latin American Mayors' Conference in Miami, where the partnership with the Belén municipality in Costa Rica began. Varun Gauri (eMBeD and codirector of the World Bank's 2015 *World Development Report* on behavioral economics, "Mind, Society, and Behavior"); Zeina Afif (eMBeD and External Communications); and Anna Fruttero (Poverty and Equity Global Practice) provided valuable comments.

The cases described in this book were possible thanks to the leadership and commitment of the respective authorities in Costa Rica, El Salvador, Guatemala, and Nicaragua. In Belén, Costa Rica, we are especially thankful to Mayor Horacio Alvarado, Manuel Alvarado (communications), Denis Mena (director of water utilities), Lorena Núñez (billing), and Sileny Rivera (adviser) for their enthusiastic leadership throughout the process. In Guatemala, the commitment of Mario Figueroa, José Roberto Ramos, and Hugo Roldán (superintendent of tax administration) was fundamental to the successful rollout of the tax pilot. In El Salvador, we owe special thanks to Edwin Segura of *La Prensa Gráfica*. In Nicaragua, the work would have not been done without the support and excellent data collection of the teams at the Ministerio de la Familia (in particular, Teresa Suazo) and the Nicaragua Center for Research in Rural and Urban Studies (in particular, Verónica Aguilera, Enoe Moncada, and the entire field team).

About the Editors and Contributors

Editors

Oscar Calvo-González is a practice manager in the World Bank's Poverty and Equity Global Practice. He was previously program leader in the Central America Department, Latin America and the Caribbean Region, where he led lending operations and analytical work on economic policy issues. Previous to his work focusing on Central America, he served as a country economist for Peru and on the country economic teams for Azerbaijan, Bolivia, and Turkey. Before joining the World Bank in 2006, he worked as a principal economist at the European Central Bank. He holds a doctorate from the London School of Economics, has published articles in refereed journals, and has edited books on wide-ranging issues such as energy subsidy reform, decentralization and public expenditure, financial stability, Spanish economic history, and foreign aid.

Laura Zoratto is a senior economist in the World Bank's Governance Global Practice, focusing on Latin America. She leads projects with national and subnational governments on the implementation and evaluation of public sector reforms, including through impact evaluations. Previously, she worked in the research department of the World Bank's Development Economics Vice Presidency, mainly on trade and competitiveness issues. Before joining the World Bank in 2011, she served as a research assistant at the University of Geneva and as an economist for the United Nations Conference on Trade and Development and DAI Brasil, among other posts. She has contributed to several publications in topics ranging from state-owned enterprises to trade cooperation and productivity. She holds a doctorate in economics from the Graduate Institute of International and Development Studies in Geneva.

Contributors

Oliver Balch is a journalist, writer, and researcher based in the United Kingdom, who specializes in sustainable development and Latin American affairs. He is a regular contributor to the *Guardian* on business and sustainability issues and is the author of three nonfiction books published by Faber & Faber: *Viva South America!* (2009), *India Rising* (2012), and *Under the Tump: Sketches of Life on the*

Welsh Borders (2016). He is a doctoral candidate at the University of Cambridge's Centre for Latin American Studies, where his research focuses on practices and discourses of corporate responsibility in the context of foreign direct investment.

Germán Caruso is an economist in the World Bank's Poverty and Equity Global Practice. His work focuses on poverty analysis and the impact of shocks and policy changes in Colombia, Côte d'Ivoire, El Salvador, and Mozambique. He has published articles in the *Journal of Development Economics*, *American Economic Review* (AER Papers and Proceedings), *Review of Income and Wealth*, *European Journal of Political Economy*, and *Climatic Change*. He holds a doctorate in economics from the University of Illinois and undergraduate and master's degrees in economics from the Universidad de San Andrés in Argentina.

Barbara Cunha is a senior economist in the World Bank's Macroeconomics and Fiscal Management Global Practice. Her work focus on the links between economic policy and growth in low- and middle-income countries (LMICs), including analysis of fiscal sustainability, efficiency of public spending, tax policy, and trade agreements. It covers a number of LMICs, including Albania, Bolivia, Brazil, Colombia, El Salvador, the former Yugoslav Republic of Macedonia, Nicaragua, and Peru. She holds a doctorate in economics from the University of Chicago and a master's degree in economics from the Fundação Getúlio Vargas in Brazil.

Matthew Darling is a vice president at ideas42, a Washington, DC–based behavioral science design and research lab, where he works across several domains including health, labor, and development. Before joining ideas42, he worked as a research assistant at the Stanford Neuroeconomics Lab and as a teaching fellow at Harvard University. He holds a master's degree in economics from Tufts University and a bachelor's degree in economics and cognitive neuroscience from Hampshire College.

Saugato Datta is a managing director at ideas42, a behavioral science research and consulting firm, where he oversees work in low- and middle-income countries, working with partners in government, nongovernmental organizations, and firms focused on low-income populations to design, test, and scale socially beneficial applications of behavioral economics. His current work spans public health, violence reduction, financial inclusion, resource conservation, agriculture, the design of transfer programs, and helping cities use behavioral science to improve urban governance and sustainability. He holds a doctorate in economics from the Massachusetts Institute of Technology and undergraduate and master's degrees in economics from the University of Cambridge and the University of Delhi.

Marco Antonio Hernández Oré is a program leader and lead economist for the Western Balkans at the World Bank, based in Austria. He previously served as a senior economist and country economist supporting countries in Africa, Europe, and Latin America. Before joining the World Bank in 2008, he worked at Charles

River Associates International and the Ministry of Finance of Peru. He holds a doctorate from Oxford University and a bachelor's degree in economics from the Massachusetts Institute of Technology.

Stewart Kettle is a senior advisor at the Behavioural Insights Team in the United Kingdom, specializing in international development. Focusing on the application of behavioral insights to public policy, he has worked with international organizations and foreign governments including the World Bank, the United Nations Development Programme, and the President's Office in Mexico. He has managed research projects, including impact evaluations, concerning interventions to increase tax collection in Guatemala and Mexico and to improve health in India and Moldova. He holds a doctorate in economics from the University of Bristol.

Karina Lorenzana is a vice president at ideas42, a behavioral science research and consulting firm, focusing on global health, the environment, and financial services. Before joining ideas42, she worked at the Clinton Foundation's Clinton Climate Initiative and the C40 Cities Climate Leadership Group in Sub-Saharan Africa and Latin America. She also served as a Peace Corps volunteer in El Salvador. She holds a master's degree in public administration from the Woodrow Wilson School of Public and International Affairs at Princeton University (with a certificate in science, technology, and environmental policy) and a bachelor's degree in international relations from Tufts University.

Karen Macours is an associate professor at the Paris School of Economics and a researcher at the French National Institute for Agricultural Research. Her current research focuses on conditional cash transfer programs, early childhood development, rural poverty, and agriculture. She has published widely in academic journals and holds a doctorate in agricultural and resource economics from the University of California, Berkeley, as well as a master's degree in agricultural engineering from the Katholieke Universiteit Leuven, Belgium.

Juan José Miranda is an environmental economist with the World Bank's Environment and Natural Resources Global Practice, where he leads analytical work on impact evaluation, conducts policy research, and provides analytical economic support on sustainable development issues. He has published in the *Journal of Environmental Economics and Management, Journal of the Association of Environmental and Resource Economists, American Journal of Political Science*, and *American Economic Review*, among others. He holds a doctorate in economics from Georgia State University.

Megan Zella Rounseville is a World Bank economist working on impact evaluations in Latin America. Previously she served in the Peace Corps in the Dominican Republic. She is also a doctoral student at the Fletcher School of Law and Diplomacy at Tufts University, focusing on development economics and impact evaluation. Her research applies econometrics to the study of poverty and inequality, child nutrition, reproductive health, access to justice, aspirations, agency, and behavioral economics. She holds a master's degree in law and diplomacy from the Fletcher School and a bachelor's degree in economics from Denison University.

Simon Ruda is a director at the Behavioural Insights Team (BIT) in the United Kingdom, where he oversees BIT's work in international development as well as in justice, security, and social integration. As a founding member of BIT, he has led some of the organization's most influential trials in public policy. With more than a decade of experience in behavioral change and public policy, he worked with every major U.K. government department and has lectured extensively on the application of behavioral science to public policy in many countries.

Manuel Sánchez Masferrer is a professor of economics at Escuela Superior de Economía y Negocios (ESEN) El Salvador and leads the Center for Social Progress, a research initiative to promote social progress measurement and policy analysis. His current work focuses on quantitative analysis of poverty and social policy, including the development of a methodology to measure multidimensional poverty in El Salvador. He has also authored three editions of the *Global Entrepreneurship Monitor* study for El Salvador. He holds a doctorate in economics from Stanford University and an undergraduate degree in economics and business from ESEN El Salvador.

Michael Sanders is chief scientist and head of research, evaluation, and social action for the Behavioural Insights Team (BIT) in the United Kingdom. His team supports BIT's policy work through the design and analysis of randomized controlled trials as well as the use of quasi-experimental methods and data science. He is an associate fellow of the Blavatnik School of Government in Oxford, where he teaches behavioral science and policy, and he is also an affiliate of the Harvard Behavioral Insights Group. He holds doctoral and master's degrees in economics, both from the University of Bristol.

Norbert Schady is a principal economic advisor for the social sector at the Inter-American Development Bank. He previously worked at the World Bank and the United Nations Children's Fund (UNICEF) and has taught at Georgetown and Princeton Universities. His main research areas include early childhood development, teacher quality, cash transfer programs, and the effects of economic crises on the accumulation of human capital. He has published three books and more than 30 articles in academic journals in economics, political science, and health, and has extensive experience advising governments in Latin America, Europe, Asia, and Africa. He holds a doctorate from Princeton University and a bachelor's degree in history from Yale University.

Kinnon Scott is a senior economist in the World Bank's Poverty and Equity Global Practice and a global lead of the Global Solutions Area on Welfare

Measurement and Capacity Building. She manages the Central America poverty team and works in-depth in Panama and Guatemala. Recently, she coauthored two Systematic Country Diagnostics and Water, Sanitation, and Hygiene Poverty Diagnostics, and she is currently working with governments on fiscal transparency and the impact of social spending on poverty. Previously, she managed the Living Standards Measurement Study Program in the Bank's Development Economics Research Group. She holds a doctorate in public and international affairs from the University of Pittsburgh.

Riccardo Trezzi is an economist at the Board of Governors of the Federal Reserve System, Research and Statistics division. His research interests lie in the fields of household finance, fiscal policy, applied econometrics, and international economics. He has published papers in refereed journals, including the *Brookings Papers on Economic Activity*, *World Bank Economic Review*, *Economic Inquiry*, and *Economic Letters*. He previously worked for the World Bank as a junior professional associate. He holds a doctorate in economics from the University of Cambridge, a master's degree in economics from the University of Warwick, and a bachelor's degree in economics from Bocconi University, Milan.

Renos Vakis is a lead economist with the World Bank's Poverty and Equity Global Practice, where he works on integrating behavioral science in the design of antipoverty policies in areas such as financial inclusion, early childhood development, social protection, health, and education. He has written extensively on poverty dynamics and mobility, risk management, social protection, and rural development and has led the design of impact evaluations of antipoverty interventions. Most recently, he has published a book on chronic poverty in Latin America and the Caribbean. He has taught economics at the School of Advanced International Studies, Johns Hopkins University. He holds doctoral and master's degrees in agricultural and resource economics from the University of California, Berkeley, and a bachelor's degree in economics from the University of California, Davis.

Abbreviations

BE	behavioral economics
BI	behavioral insights
BIT	Behavioural Insights Team (United Kingdom)
CCT	conditional cash transfer
FMLN	Farabundo Martí National Liberation Front (*Frente Farabundo Martí Para La Liberación Nacional*) (El Salvador)
GDP	gross domestic product
LMICs	low- and middle-income countries
LPG	liquefied petroleum gas
MIFAMILIA	Ministry of the Family (Nicaragua)
RCT	randomized control trial
SAT	Guatemalan Tax Authority (*Superintendencia de Administración Tributaria*)
SMS	short message service
WDR 2015	*World Development Report 2015: Mind, Society, and Behavior*
£	British pound
C	Costa Rican colón
US$	U.S. dollar

Overview

Oscar Calvo-González and Laura Zoratto

Introduction

Imagine you are the mayor of a small municipality. You know that your city will face water scarcity in the medium term. You think of increasing the local supply of water, but that requires resources you don't have. You've tried raising water prices to curb demand, but the limited price increases that the law permitted had little impact. You notice water is still being wasted—what can you do about it? This is the dilemma that Horacio Alvarado, the mayor of Belén, Costa Rica, faced. He had also tried putting billboards in his municipality encouraging people to conserve water but had little success.

This type of problem is well known by government officials worldwide. Often, traditional tools such as regulations and incentives are not available to solve the problem: they either take too much time to be deployed—because they may require lengthy approvals by Congress, in the case of legislation—or they are insufficient to achieve the desired change. Authorities often feel that power is increasingly "harder to use," to borrow the expression of political analyst Moisés Naím (2013). This book presents examples of simple, behaviorally informed approaches that have been applied to deal with this type of problem, complementing the set of traditional tools available to governments. These cases build upon and reflect the more recent literature on behavioral economics and its applications to public policy (Ariely 2008; Datta and Mullainathan 2014; Dolan et al. 2012; Halpern 2005; Haynes, Goldacre, and Torgerson 2012; Kahneman 2003; Mullainathan and Shafir 2013; Thaler and Sunstein 2008; World Bank 2015).

This book brings together a set of experiences from Central American countries. In each case, behavioral insights are applied to different areas of public policy, all within a development context. These experiences collectively show the promise of public policies that are informed by a better understanding of what drives individuals' behavior.[1] In Costa Rica, informing households about how much water they consume relative to their neighbors reduced water consumption by nearly 5 percent per month, on average (chapter 1). In Guatemala, altering the way government communicates with taxpayers increased revenue collection (chapter 2). As further discussed below, the Guatemalan approach also achieved substantial results with Costa Rican taxpayers. These examples illustrate the possibility of using nontraditional tools, complementary to regulation, in a context where time and resources are limited.

Framing the Problem

Let's go back to Belén, the small municipality in Costa Rica referred to above. The World Bank invited Horacio Alvarado, Belén's mayor, along with other mayors from across Latin America to a brainstorming session in June 2013. An exercise asked the mayors to identify problems they faced in their municipalities but to refrain from assumptions about the underlying causes or appropriate solutions. Instead, the mayors were asked to define the problems by simply filling in the gaps in the following statements: "People are doing _____. We want people to do _____." Such an exercise frames the problem in terms of individual behavioral patterns. In doing so, it reveals how many assumptions we make about the cause of a given problem, which in turns limits the range of solutions we can think of. By reframing common policy problems, the brainstorming aimed to get closer to "question zero"—the core of the problem.

The Power of Examples

The exercise was powerful also because of the use of examples. In addition to the brainstorming, the mayors were presented with a variety of cases where public authorities had adopted innovative solutions that drew on behavioral insights. The goal was to shift how they think about common problems through the use of examples, thereby releasing the potential for fresh thinking and policy innovation. An intriguing finding from the literature on innovation suggests that many innovations happen by adapting an existing practice for a different purpose—a process known as exaptation. Furthermore, this process is shown to be incremental. We were deliberate in our effort to harness this dynamic, which quickly revealed itself in practice.

For instance, the idea of focusing on water consumption in Belén occurred to Alvarado after he heard about a South African ministry that was trying to reduce electricity consumption by finding ways to alert employees about the consequences of their actions. "I don't have that problem in Belén. People don't leave the lights on, but they leave the taps on," Alvarado said. Later, he learned about water savings achieved in the U.S. state of Georgia through the use of "nudge" messages on household water bills. This convinced Alvarado to adopt a similar approach in his municipality. The use of examples in our brainstorming exercise helped one idea lead to another.

The power of examples was also crucial in the rollout of the Guatemala tax compliance case. It all started when we learned in 2012 about the Behavioural Insights Team (BIT) and, in particular, their successful experiment to raise tax collection in the United Kingdom (BIT 2012). We started to work with the BIT on tax collection in Guatemala. Together, we were able to help Guatemala raise tax revenues by highlighting to taxpayers that most of their fellow citizens paid their taxes. The experiment has since been replicated in Costa Rica and Poland as part of World Bank engagements. In Costa Rica, the pilot demonstrated that enforcement e-mails sent to non-tax filers significantly increased compliance with the income tax and did not crowd out compliance with other taxes. The e-mails approximately tripled the income tax declaration rate and doubled the payment rate.

Looking at development issues through a behavioral insights lens can be informative even in cases where the original challenge was not initially framed around behavioral change. This occurred with the Nicaraguan cash transfer program, Atención a Crisis. The analysis of the program's impact, further discussed in chapter 3, found that children in households randomly assigned to receive benefits had significantly higher levels of cognitive development nine months after the program began (Macours, Schady, and Vakis 2012). However, the authors found that the cash transfer was not the only explanation for this positive impact. The influence of parental behavioral change, which emerged in response to nonmonetary factors such as increased social interactions and motivation, was felt as well. This insight has led to new efforts to make the most of these findings. In Nicaragua, for example, an ongoing trial uses short message service (SMS) technology to send information to parents in 4,000 households. The trial aims to change key behavior patterns and thereby improve child welfare. The treatment combines variations as to who receives the messages, what type of information is provided, and how that information is presented.

The Empirical Investigation

We conducted randomized control trials (RCTs) under rigorous testing conditions in three of our interventions (tax compliance in Guatemala, water conservation in Costa Rica, and early childhood development in Nicaragua). RCTs are powerful tools for attributing results to a behaviorally informed policy, but they are only one of several ways of incorporating behavioral concepts in our work. Understanding perceptions, biases, and mental models can also help us understand the unintended effects of a policy, as the following two examples from El Salvador illustrate.

Effects of Perceptions, Biases, and Mental Models
When working on a major gas subsidy reform in El Salvador, we were faced with a puzzle: many of the beneficiaries of the reform were against it. Further investigation into people's perceptions of the reform revealed that lack of information was critical to how they viewed the reform (chapter 4). Our empirical investigation set out to answer two specific research questions: What factors drove the unpopularity of the reform before and after its implementation? And what factors accounted for the reform's relatively high popularity two years after it

was implemented? Overall, the findings suggest that actions to increase the information provided to individuals could have affected their level of satisfaction with the reform. Such efforts could have played a role without necessarily modifying the content of the reform. This finding indicates that, when seeking to understand the success or failure of policy reforms, policy makers would do well to explore factors that may affect why an individual considers himself or herself to be a winner or a loser of those reforms.

Chapter 5 also uses behavioral insights to analyze subsidy reforms in El Salvador, in a different context and with a different methodology. It describes a set of economic behavioral games designed to evaluate the willingness of high-income householders to accept subsidy reforms that would affect them directly. Results suggest that most of the well-to-do are prepared to see their electricity and water subsidies reduced if the economic gains of these reductions were to be used for poverty reduction projects or for the delivery of public goods. Furthermore, information about the regressive nature of the present subsidy was shown to positively affect the present beneficiaries' willingness to share, or forgo, their subsidy.

World Development Report 2015 in Action

These cases illustrate some of the findings of *World Development Report 2015: Mind, Society, and Behavior* (*WDR 2015*) in practice.[2] *WDR 2015* challenges the assumption that we are rational choice makers and presents three principles of human decision making and its interactions with policy (World Bank 2015): namely, humans think socially, automatically, and with mental models. People make most judgments and most choices automatically, not deliberatively.

In the case of the gas subsidy reform in El Salvador, for example, we see this automatic thinking in the form of negativity bias. The negative perception among the population at large—even among those who would benefit monetarily from the reform—was set in people's minds before the changes were implemented. The reform entailed moving away from selling gas bottles at a subsidized price to selling the bottles at an unsubsidized price but compensating households by transferring the amount of the subsidy every month to households, mainly through the electricity bill. In other words, most households would end up receiving a discount on their electricity bill that was the same or greater than the subsidy they were previously receiving at the point of sale. Most Salvadoran households would benefit from the reform, because they would now get the amount of the subsidy even in months when they didn't buy a bottle of gas. Yet, even among these households that gained from the change in the subsidy mechanism, the majority disapproved of the reform.

How can we explain the puzzle that a reform's "winners" feel as if they are "losers"? As further discussed in chapter 4, a key factor behind this puzzle is the effect of insufficient information and the knowledge vacuum this creates for people. When we asked people about the gas subsidy reform, those who self-identified as ill-informed easily came up with potentially negative consequences of the reform. They were harder pressed than the better-informed to think up potentially positive consequences. Our econometric analysis shows that this negativity bias is influenced by the level of information that individuals receive. Being better informed mitigated this negativity bias.

Significantly, the surveyed population expressed a view about the gas subsidy reform regardless of the level of information available to them. This is an example of automatic thinking that draws on a default assumption. These assumptions result from specific mental models. In a context where institutions have limited credibility and the public does not trust them, one can expect that the default assumption will not necessarily be positive. This is what we saw with El Salvador's gas subsidy reform: those who had less information had a more negative view of the reform.

Individuals in a given society share a common perspective on how to make sense of the world around them and how to understand themselves. This in turn helps them make decisions in daily life. Following the framework proposed by *WDR 2015*, this process has become known as thinking with mental models. Such models provide us with default assumptions about the people and institutions that we interact with—whether it's the government that is collecting taxes, for example, or state administrators who are implementing a given policy reform. If our default assumption is a negative one, the challenge for the policy maker is all the more difficult.

But mental models affect much more than the public's perception of government. Consider again the gas subsidy reform in El Salvador: When we asked about the pros and cons of the new subsidy delivery method, survey respondents often complained that the subsidy was no longer linked to gas consumption. Curiously, they also interpreted the flexibility afforded to them by the new reform (namely, the ability to use the dollar amount of the subsidy for whatever they chose) as a negative feature rather than a positive one. This presents a clear example of "mental accounting," whereby individuals earmark some income toward certain expenditures. The *WDR 2015* findings also enhance our understanding of how collective behaviors—such as widespread mistrust in governments—develop and become entrenched in a society.

Moreover, how people act and think is often influenced by the behaviors and thinking patterns of those around them: in other words, we think socially. In the case of water consumption in Belén, Costa Rica, the peer comparison provides an example. For example, when one particular resident received a water bill with a frowny face on it (indicating that he had consumed more water than his neighbors), the individual called the municipality to complain. He knew for a fact that his next-door neighbor used more water than he did, he argued. On learning that the comparison was with the whole neighborhood and not just his immediate neighbor, he said he would be more attentive to his water consumption in the future! The same applies to tax collection in Guatemala: when individual taxpayers were made aware of the tax-paying behaviors of others, they altered their own behaviors, and tax collection rates went up.

Large Impacts from Small Details

These cases also illustrate the importance of paying close attention to both the design and the implementation details of reforms. Government actions frequently have unintended consequences that minimize or derail achievement of a policy's end goals. Often a minor and overlooked detail gets in the way. For the same reason, small additions or alterations in the design can sometimes substantially improve project outcomes. In the case of water consumption in Belén, for instance, the provision of household water consumption data made a difference in household consumption patterns. In Guatemala, tinkering with the language and format of the standard letter from the tax authority helped to increase tax payments. The disproportionate impact that small changes in design and user experience can have on project outcomes represents one of the critical lessons from this book.

That small details matter implies that we first need to deliberately seek out users and understand their perspective. In practice, this means closely examining how people interact with the government, paying attention to what they are doing as opposed to what we expect them to do, and constantly interrogating our assumptions.[3] Such an inquiry is best undertaken through mixed methods of qualitative and quantitative work. In Costa Rica, we achieved this through focus groups among Belén citizens. We learned, for example, that many residents not only understood the importance of conserving water but also were predisposed to act on this understanding. The same residents, however, were unaware of how much water they were consuming (both in overall terms and in relative terms) or how to significantly reduce their water consumption. Similarly, the focus groups informed us that some consumers were unaware of how constrained the water supply really is. This is understandable (albeit incorrect) given the abundant rainfall and lush vegetation in Costa Rica.

How can an approach that relies on relatively small details result in large impacts? How can small interventions have economic significance? In some cases, gains that appear small are actually relatively large when one considers the difficulty of achieving similar-size impacts through alternative means. In Guatemala, a simple change in the letters sent to taxpayers generated a substantial increase in tax collection rates. In Belén, water consumption decreased by 5 percent—a large drop in terms of water consumption compared with other efforts. During a severe drought in North Carolina in 2007, for example, a drastic mandatory policy restricting all water use outdoors generated a 13 percent drop in water consumption (Wichman 2016). Moreover, relative to price mechanisms, water conservation initiatives unrelated to prices—such as the exercise with messages in the water bills—induce more equitable effects across income classes. In contrast, as in Belén, residential water price increases fall more heavily on lower-income households while failing to reduce consumption among households with higher nonessential water use (Wichman, Taylor, and von Haefen 2016).

One of the main attractions of behavior-influenced interventions is their low cost. Unlike traditional development projects, they typically do not require high up-front investment in infrastructure or information systems, nor are significant additional human resources necessary. Instead, they seek to work within established systems and use existing resources. One clear advantage of this approach is that project sponsors can take action with a small or even nonexistent budget. It is no coincidence, for example, that the creation of the BIT in the United Kingdom coincided with a period of economic recession and government-led austerity.[4] The unit had no independent budget to implement projects. Indeed, given the general context of resource scarcity, its ability to assure government ministries that its approaches would be cost-neutral or better proved critical in gaining buy-in. Relative to their low cost, however, behavior-influenced interventions can deliver considerable potential returns.

The Sustainability of Behavioral Change

Naturally, questions remain about the impact of behavior-oriented interventions in the medium and long term. It is likely that a range of different policy interventions over the longer term will be needed, with behaviorally informed strategies representing just one intervention among many. One major issue, for instance, centers on the sustainability of behavioral changes. Some interventions may promote a shift in behavioral patterns in the immediate term but fail to change underlying attitudes and motivations. In such cases, the sustainability of change is usually reduced. When the "nudge" is removed, individuals have a propensity to return to their previous habits.

Longer-term impacts rely on changing people's preferences. This can be achieved by fostering social norms or influencing attitudes, for example. In such cases, behaviorally informed interventions generally have to run over an extended period or simply be incorporated into day-to-day business. For instance, in Guatemala and Costa Rica, the letters sent to taxpayers and consumers, respectively, were modified after the experiment to incorporate the changes proposed by the intervention. In Guatemala, the government decided to scale up the pilot nationally in 2014 and continues to work with the World Bank on conducting new experiments across all major types of taxes. In the case of Belén, Costa Rica, we show that the intervention, implemented only once, generated a decrease in water consumption in the following four months. The introduction of messages in water bills three or four times a year, or every month, could potentially further decrease water consumption or generate a permanent change in behavior. This remains an empirical question for further investigation.

Contributions of This Volume

Taken together, the cases in this volume demonstrate the practical implications of applying behavioral insights and their relevance for development work. Interest in this topic is not only intellectual, but has practical applications as well. The World Bank has a growing number of projects aiming to test the impact of interventions informed by behavioral insights, ranging from efforts to help change handwashing habits to improving kids' noncognitive skills. However, these still represent a small number.

When developing any project, we typically identify the beneficiaries, the expected outcomes, and the desired behavior change. That said, this last element is not always given due consideration. A recent analysis of the Bank's project delivery challenges and success factors (Gonzalez Asis and Woolcock 2015) turned up few references to behavior change. In only a couple of cases were behavior components mentioned as having provided a fundamental contribution to the intervention's success. In contrast, focusing on desired behavior changes was precisely the approach underpinning the country cases reported in this book, with all activities sharing an emphasis on testing and learning.

This short book concludes with some reflections on the lessons learned from these cases. These include reflections on how we first engaged with our counterparts and identified issues with a strong behavioral component, how we implemented the pilot projects and managed associated challenges, and how we monitored outcomes and analyzed results. We hope these experiences will help to inform others about the potential of applying behavioral insights in a development context and encourage them to consider such approaches as a complement to traditional policy measures.

Summaries of the Chapters

The first three chapters present results from three interventions that explored simple nudges to elicit the conservation of water, greater compliance in the payment of taxes, and parental behaviors that enhance child development, respectively:

- *Chapter 1, "A Behavioral Approach to Water Conservation: Evidence from Costa Rica,"* describes behavioral interventions designed to help municipal authorities motivate homeowners in a high-income district of Costa Rica to reduce their water use. The strategies are split between a "descriptive norm" approach (whereby homeowners are encouraged to compare their consumption with that of their neighbors and the city as a whole) and a "plan-making" approach (which pushes homeowners to set clear measures and goals for modifying their water use habits). Two of those strategies (one "descriptive norm" strategy and one "plan-making" strategy) succeeded, generating water reductions of 3.4–5.5 percent in the following month.

- *Chapter 2, "Promoting Tax Compliance in Guatemala using Behavioral Economics: Evidence from Two Randomized Trials,"* describes interventions for a country where tax revenues average about 12 percent of gross domestic product (GDP), less than half the regional average for Latin America. Drawing on insights from behavioral science, we implemented a nationwide letter-based experiment to increase compliance among nonpaying individuals and firms. The RCT was structured around four treatments using behavioral design. All the letters showed positive results, with two markedly increasing the rates of income tax declaration and payment. These high-performing treatments were based on (a) a deterrent message, which framed nondeclaration as an intentional and deliberate choice; and (b) a social norms message, which showed nonpaying taxpayers that they were in the minority. Together, they helped more than triple tax receipts among the target group. Their effects were still noticeable on taxpayers' behavior 12 months after the pilot.

- *Chapter 3, "Enhancing Child Development through Changes to Parental Behaviors: Using Conditional Cash Transfers in Nicaragua,"* illustrates the usefulness of thinking beyond simple nudges when applying behavioral insights to public policy. It describes a rare long-term study of the Nicaragua cash transfer program, Attention to Crisis (Atención a Crisis), that rigorously examined the mechanisms evoking behavioral change. The analysis of this program's impact on early childhood cognitive development found that children in households randomly assigned to receive cash benefits had significantly higher development outcomes nine months after the program began. However, the cash transfer mechanism was not the only explanation for this positive impact: nonmonetary channels such as increased social interactions and motivation also evoked behavioral change in parents.

Next, chapters 4 and 5 examine energy subsidy reform in El Salvador from a behavioral angle using two different methods—an analysis based on household survey data and a game-based subsidy reform simulation:

- *Chapter 4, "When Winners Feel Like Losers: Evidence from an Energy Subsidy Reform,"* presents an analysis of El Salvador's 2011 gas subsidy reform, which proved unpopular even though it benefited most of the population, especially those on low incomes. Using ad hoc household surveys from before and after the reform's implementation, the chapter seeks to explain this apparent anomaly. Using probit/logit models, it shows that the provision of information is critical to individuals' opinions of the reform measure. Political partisanship and subsequent experience during the implementation phase also influence public opinion. The analysis suggests that, for other areas of reform, policy makers may need to look beyond a consideration of the reform's winners and losers to ascertain satisfaction levels.

- *Chapter 5, "Redistribution in Times of Fiscal Pressure: Using Games to Inform a Subsidy Reform in El Salvador,"* takes an experimental approach to the same topic, exploring the insights gained from a game-based simulation of a subsidy reform. It adds to previous research mainly by considering two factors: the impact that the destination of subsidy funds has on people's willingness to forgo a subsidy, and the role of that information in influencing how willing people are to share. The chapter also considers how individual beliefs about government feed into acceptance levels for subsidy reform—an issue that featured prominently in chapter 4. Results suggest that most people are prepared to see their electricity and water subsidies decrease if the economic gains of these reductions are used for poverty reduction projects or for the delivery of public goods. Furthermore, information about the regressive nature of the current subsidy was shown to positively affect the beneficiaries' willingness to share, or forgo, their subsidy.

This final chapter distills some of the lessons learned during the preparation and implementation of the pilot interventions reported throughout this book:

- *Chapter 6, "Lessons Learned from Implementing Behaviorally Informed Pilots,"* reflects on the progress made in applying behavioral insights in a development context, which has proved to be a fertile ground for behaviorally informed interventions. The success of such pilots is evidence that the application of behavioral insights for development is a promising avenue for the future.

Notes

1. A word on terminology is warranted. When we set out to undertake these activities in Central America, we chose the expression "behaviorally informed public policy" to make the point that although "nudges" are an important tool, they are not the only way in which public policy can be behaviorally informed. Since we started our work in Central America, the literature has advanced in clarifying and classifying the terminology. "Behavioral insights applied to policy" has emerged as a clearer label for our approach, and the distinction between "behavioral economics," "nudges," and "behavioral insights" is now more precise. The 2016 European Commission report on the topic distinguishes clearly between behavioral insights (BI) and nudges (Lourenço et al. 2016): "[A] nudge is an easy and often low-cost intervention . . . that modifies the choice architecture, altering people's behavior in a predictable way, while preserving the same range of choice options. By contrast, BIs represent an input to the policy process, and can be fully integrated with and inform other traditional forms of intervention (i.e., regulations, incentives, information requirements). In this sense, BIs may support a broader range of policy instruments. . . . BIs, contrarily to nudges, do not warrant a specific type of output, and indeed sometimes suggest that no intervention, or a conventional one, is the best solution."

2. Since the release of *WDR 2015*, the World Bank has created the Mind, Behavior, and Development (eMBeD) Unit within the Poverty and Equity Global Practice.

3. Gonzalez Asis and Woolcock (2015) identify five core principles of the science of delivery that resonate well with the experience from our cases. Among these principles, they note that identifying the incentives that motivate behaviors and integrating these findings into design and implementation of delivery solutions is crucial for reaching project outcomes.

4. Accounts of the creation of the Behavioural Insights Team and its early work can be found in Halpern (2015) and Service and Gallagher (2017). The BIT's current and recent interventions are described on the BIT website: http://www.behaviouralinsights.co.uk/.

References

Ariely, Dan. 2008. *Predictably Irrational: The Hidden Forces that Shape Our Decisions.* New York: HarperCollins Publishers.

Datta, Saugato, and Sendhil Mullainathan. 2014. "Behavioral Design: A New Approach to Development Policy." *Review of Income and Wealth* 60 (1): 7–35.

Dolan, Paul, Michael Hallsworth, David Halpern, Dominic King, Robert Metcalfe, and Ivo Vlaev. 2012. "Influencing Behaviour: The Mindspace Way." *Journal of Economic Psychology* 33 (1): 264–77.

Gonzalez Asis, Maria, and Michael Woolcock. 2015. "Operationalizing the Science of Delivery Agenda to Enhance Development Results." Framework paper, Report No. 103170, World Bank, Washington, DC.

Halpern, David. 2005. *Social Capital.* Cambridge: Polity Press.

———. 2015. *Inside the Nudge Unit: How Small Changes Can Make a Big Difference.* London: W. H. Allen.

Haynes, Laura, Ben Goldacre, and David Torgerson. 2012. "Test, Learn, Adapt: Developing Public Policy with Randomised Controlled Trials." Policy paper, Cabinet Office Behavioural Insights Team, London.

Kahneman, Daniel. 2003. "A Perspective on Judgment and Choice: Mapping Bounded Rationality." *American Psychologist* 58 (9): 487–504.

Lourenço, Joana Sousa, Emanuele Ciriolo, Sara Rafael Almeida, and Xavier Troussard. 2016. *Behavioural Insights Applied to Policy: European Report 2016.* Brussels: European Union.

Macours, Karen, Norbert Schady, and Renos Vakis. 2012. "Cash Transfers, Behavioral Changes, and Cognitive Development in Early Childhood: Evidence from a Randomized Experiment." *American Economic Journal: Applied Economics* 4 (2): 247–73.

Mullainathan, Sendhil, and Eldar Shafir. 2013. *Scarcity: Why Having Too Little Means So Much.* New York: Times Books, Henry Holt & Company LLC.

Naím, Moisés. 2013. *The End of Power: From Boardrooms to Battlefields and Churches to States, Why Being in Charge Isn't What It Used to Be.* New York: Basic Books.

Service, Owain, and Rory Gallagher. 2017. *Think Small: The Surprisingly Simple Ways to Reach Big Goals.* London: Michael O'Mara Books Limited.

Thaler, Richard H., and Cass R. Sunstein. 2008. *Nudge: Improving Decisions about Health, Wealth, and Happiness.* New Haven, CT: Yale University Press.

Wichman, Casey. 2016. "Effective Water Demand Management: Prices vs. Restrictions." *Resources for the Future* (blog), March 16. http://www.rff.org/blog/2016/effective -water-demand-management-prices-vs-restrictions.

Wichman, Casey, Laura Taylor, and Roger von Haefen. 2016. "Conservation Policies: Who Responds to Price and Who Responds to Prescription?" *Journal of Environmental Economics and Management* 79 (C): 114–34.

World Bank. 2015. *World Development Report 2015: Mind, Society, and Behavior.* Washington, DC: World Bank.

CHAPTER 1

A Behavioral Approach to Water Conservation: Evidence from Costa Rica

Saugato Datta, Juan José Miranda, Laura Zoratto,
Oscar Calvo-González, Matthew Darling, and Karina Lorenzana

Introduction

Water scarcity is fast becoming one of this century's high-priority public policy concerns (Ferraro and Price 2013). The effects of factors such as population growth, increased urbanization, and climate change have led the United Nations to predict that more than two-thirds of the world's population will reside in regions considered water-stressed by 2025 (UNDP 2006). Given the surging demand for water in cities, many municipal governments in low- and middle-income countries (LMICs) find themselves struggling to provide reliable access to drinking water, sewerage, and wastewater treatment (Foster 2005). In Latin America, the recent introduction of water rationing in populous cities such as São Paulo in Brazil (Scanzerla 2014) and Bogotá in Colombia (*El Tiempo* 2014) provide a taste of the policy challenges ahead.

Although Latin America is home to 31 percent of the world's freshwater resources, the region's capacity to increase supply is limited. As a consequence, policy interventions typically focus on demand management. For many municipal governments, reducing household water consumption is a priority, because this is where per capita use rates are highest. Current strategies for doing so include water price or tax increases as well as public awareness campaigns about water scarcity and the need for water conservation.

The mountainous topography of Costa Rica makes it a water-rich nation. Yet with water demand and water supply roughly balanced at present, the country's population of just over 4.4 million people is facing a possible water deficit in the near future. Indeed, shortages and rationing of water are already occurring in several parts of the country (Aguilar 2014).

This chapter is adapted from Datta, S., J. J. Miranda, L. Zoratto, O. Calvo-González, M. Darling, and K. Lorenzana. 2015. "A Behavioral Approach to Water Conservation: Evidence from Costa Rica." Policy Research Working Paper 7283, World Bank, Washington, DC.

As home to three in every five Costa Ricans, cities will play a vital part in how the country's water management story plays out. Most urban households are now connected to water supply systems (99 percent), but almost one-fifth of homes (18 percent) lack consistent access (Bower 2014). Responsibility for water provision in Costa Rica is divided between municipal water departments and the national water system operator, the Costa Rican Institute of Aqueducts and Sewers (Instituto Costarricense de Acueductos y Alcantarillados, or AyA).

Our pilot experiment took place in Belén, a district of San Juan that consists of three municipalities: Asunción, La Rivera, and San Antonio (map 1.1). The neighborhood is home to just over 6,000 dwellings and has a population of around 21,600 people.[1] Average water consumption in Belén is 27 cubic meters per month, 1.25 times the national average of approximately 22 cubic meters per month (Municipality of Belén 2010). If current water use behaviors

Map 1.1 Vicinity of Belén, Costa Rica

Source: World Bank staff.

remain unchanged and no additional production or investments are made, the area is likely to face water shortages by the end of the next decade.

Policy Options to Face a Looming Water Deficit

Policy Tools to Reduce Water Consumption

Broadly speaking, policy makers in urban municipalities such as Belén can attempt to reduce household water consumption through nonpecuniary measures such as raising awareness and pecuniary steps such as price increases.

The most widespread nonpecuniary measures center on communications and education campaigns. These typically employ media platforms such as radio broadcasts and billboards. Such campaigns don't discriminate among consumers on the basis of their ability to pay. This approach avoids the negative associations that people feel toward price-based interventions, but the effectiveness of broad-based campaigns is open to question. In Belén, for example, experiments with this approach have not proved successful.

Other nonpecuniary measures include water rationing or restrictions on particular types or times of water use. "Hosepipe bans" on outdoor water use during dry periods are commonplace in the United Kingdom, for instance. Strict compliance and monitoring requirements mean these interventions only really work on a short-term, emergency basis. They can also have unintended consequences. Water rationing often hits the poor the hardest, for example. Because they can't afford water storage devices such as water tanks, they end up having to purchase expensive drinking water from private suppliers.

Pecuniary instruments represent an imperfect tool as well. First, it's difficult to increase water prices. Governments in LMICs typically set the water price to keep low-income households from being priced out of the market. Second, even when price increases are feasible, they aren't as effective as expected because price elasticity of demand for water is often low, especially for wealthy users (Ferraro and Miranda 2013; Olmstead, Hanemann, and Stavins 2007). Recent research suggests this could be because individuals may fail to notice taxes or price increases, especially when they are not charged at the point of sale (Chetty, Looney, and Kroft 2009). This was the case in Belén, where a 100 percent price hike in November 2012 resulted in only a 15 percent decrease in water use (and then only for one month, before it bounced back to higher-than-previous levels).

Behavioral Interventions for Water Conservation

Given the limitations of standard price- or communications-based approaches, identifying alternatives has emerged as a research and policy priority. Behavioral economics presents one avenue for such alternatives. The main attraction of this cognitive-based approach lies in its promise to change behavior without necessarily resorting to price-based interventions or moral suasion (Datta and Mullainathan 2014).

Trials in other areas, particularly those relating to energy consumption, indicate that peer-comparison based approaches (also known as "social norm" interventions) hold the greatest potential for water conservation. Some initial experiments in social norm messaging by water utilities have resulted in reductions in water use of around 5 percent (Ferraro and Price 2013). Similar approaches by hotels to limit towel washing have demonstrated comparable results (Goldstein, Cialdini, and Griskevicius 2008).

The use of such behavioral tools in the LMIC context—such as in Belén, Costa Rica—remains rare. This is the case in all sectors, not just water.

Intervention Design

The current experiment tested three behavioral interventions to reduce water consumption in Belén (box 1.1). Belén is a high-income municipality in the Costa Rican capital. We chose Belén as a test site because it is an area of above-average water use and because it has proved largely immune to conventional attempts to reduce water consumption.

We applied the intervention to 5,626 households, all of which are individually metered. The households were randomly assigned to one of three treatments and a control group.

Two of the treatment groups were subject to a "social norm" approach based on peer comparisons: In the first case, households were prompted to compare their water use with that of the average household in their local neighborhood. (Belén has six neighborhoods as a whole.) In the other case, the average for the city as a whole was used as a comparable. We hypothesized that people's response rate would be affected inversely by the perceived social distance from the particular reference group (either their neighborhood or the city of Belén).

The third intervention was based on a "plan-making" principle. This involved the use of a planning prompt (Rogers et al. 2013) to help people set personal goals and create concrete plans to reduce their water consumption.

Rationale for Interventions

Insights supporting the experiment came from both the literature on behavioral interventions and from four focus groups of Belén residents held in March 2014. The focus groups revealed a number of key insights about residents' attitudes toward water use. The most striking was the disinclination of residents to reduce their water use despite agreeing that conserving water is important. They believed their own water use was "justified" (because they paid their bills) or "inevitable" (because their water needs were high). We therefore thought that

---

Box 1.1 Three Behavioral Interventions to Reduce Water Consumption in Belén

- *Neighborhood comparison:* The treatment group was informed how their consumption compared with that of the average household in their neighborhood.
- *City comparison:* The treatment group was informed how their consumption compared with that of the average household in Belén.
- *Plan making:* The treatment group was made aware of their relative consumption and prompted to establish concrete steps to reduce it.

---

an approach that encouraged a personalized, concrete intention to save water would be more useful than increasing awareness about water conservation.

The focus groups also highlighted the difficulty many residents had in deciphering their monthly bills. Although the bills made it clear how much their water consumption cost, they didn't make it easy for homeowners to identify the *amount* of water they used (figure 1.1). To engage residents, we realized that their own water use had to become salient to them.

Figure 1.1 Municipal Water Bill in Belén, Costa Rica

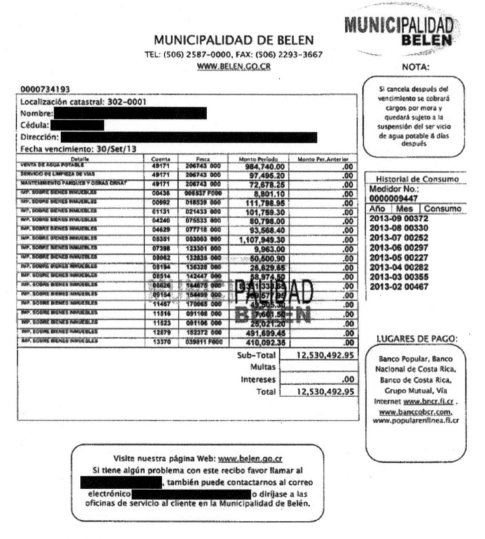

Source: Municipality of Belén.

Note: Water usage appears in the small box at the right side of the bill, under "Historial de Consumo." The large box dominating the bill presents the value to be paid.

A related problem that emerged from our initial research was the inability of people in Belén to objectively evaluate their water use. They didn't know whether it was too high or whether it was reasonable, for instance. We therefore resolved that introducing a suitable benchmark against which households could measure their own water use would be a helpful step. The literature on peer norms substantiates this.

Finally, it became clear that most people weren't very aware of what practical steps they could take to reduce their water consumption. This is partly because they had little sense of how resource-intensive common activities actually were—such as watering lawns and washing cars. For this reason, we surmised that giving specific guidance would have more effect than issuing a general exhortation for people to change their water use.

Design Features

In light of the bottlenecks highlighted by the focus groups, we felt it was necessary to identify a suitable benchmark for comparison purposes and to counter residents' lack of clarity or sense of significance about their own water use.

As such, we adopted an approach based on simple stickers. Depending on residents' level of water consumption, their monthly water bill displayed a brightly colored sticker with either a "smiley face" (if their use was below the median) or a "frowny face" (if it was above the median). In addition to the visual illustration, the sticker came with a message either congratulating the homeowners for using less water or alerting them to their high consumption. This approach was used in the first two treatments: the "neighborhood comparison" and the "city comparison" (figures 1.2 and 1.3, respectively).

For the plan-making intervention, we sent households a worksheet printed on a postcard along with their monthly bill (figure 1.4). Included on the worksheet was a prompt to enter their water consumption, thus making it salient. The piece of paper also included the average water use of a Belén household, which provided a benchmark. The residents were asked to write this down as well. Instructions on the postcard then encouraged people to establish a personal goal for reducing their water use and to check one or more of six listed tips for using less water, such as turning off the faucet while brushing their teeth.

We favored simple interventions that did not require elaborate software or expensive technologies to implement. Belén shares the same technological constraints that affect many municipalities in LMICs. For this reason, we chose not to print personalized bills with messages about relative consumption. Instead, our interventions required the Municipality of Belén simply to print out various colored stickers and worksheets. The staff members in charge of stuffing bills into envelopes were then given access to a spreadsheet that indicated which sticker or postcard to use with each bill, following the randomization strategy described in the next section.

Figure 1.2 Sticker Design for Norm-Based Water Use Intervention: Belén Neighborhood Comparison

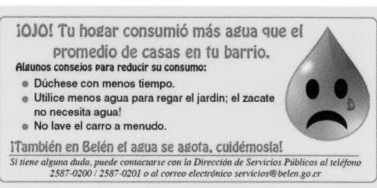

Source: © World Bank. Permission required for reuse.
Note: Blue sticker says, "Water is scarce even in Belén, let's take care of it! Your house consumed less water than the average home in your neighborhood! Good job!" Yellow sticker says, "Look out! Your house consumed more water than the average home in your neighborhood. Some tips to reduce your consumption: Take shorter showers. Use less water for the lawn; lawn does not need water! Wash cars less frequently. Water is scarce even in Belén, let's take care of it!"

Implementation

We drew our sample from a list of active residential water consumers in Belén in April 2014.[2] Each household belongs to one of 25 "postal routes," which determines when they receive their monthly bill. As well as stratifying participating households by neighborhood and average monthly consumption, we also stratified them by postal route. The households were then divided randomly into three treatment groups and a control group.

The first treatment arm ($n = 1,399$) received the "neighborhood comparison" treatment. The second treatment arm ($n = 1,399$) received the "city comparison" treatment. The third treatment arm ($n = 1,399$) received the "plan-making" intervention. The control group ($n = 1,429$) received no additional information during

Figure 1.3 Sticker Design for Norm-Based Water Use Intervention: Belén Citywide Comparison

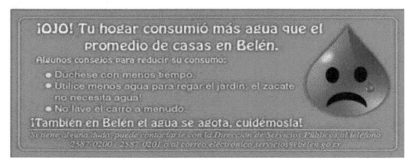

Source: © World Bank. Permission required for reuse.
Note: Green sticker says, "Water is scarce even in Belén, let's take care of it! Your house consumed less water than the average house in your city! Good job!" Red sticker says, "Look out! Your house consumed more water than the average house in your city. Some tips to reduce your consumption: Take shorter showers. Use less water for the lawn; lawn does not need water! Wash cars less frequently. Water is scarce even in Belén, let's take care of it!"

the experiment and continued to receive a utility bill without a sticker or post-card. The final number of households in the experiment was slightly smaller, because a June 2014 change in Belén's billing meters forced us to drop some households from the experiment.[3]

We implemented the interventions during the July 2014 billing cycle in Belén. This was when households received water bills based on their water consumption in the 31-day period before this bill was generated.

We call our postintervention consumption variables "August 2014 Billed Consumption" and "September 2014 Billed Consumption." All the bills cover water use in the 31-day period before the bills' generation. However, the month on the bill varies because the bills are not all sent out together.[4] Because of this potential crossover, we took bills covering a two-month period after the intervention as the basis for our outcome data. The results therefore refer to the mean average for residents' billed consumption in August and September 2014. As a baseline, we used water consumption rates in the previous wet or rainy season. This runs from May through November and therefore covers both the implementation and postintervention periods.

Figure 1.4 Worksheet Design for "Plan-Making" Water Use Intervention in Belén

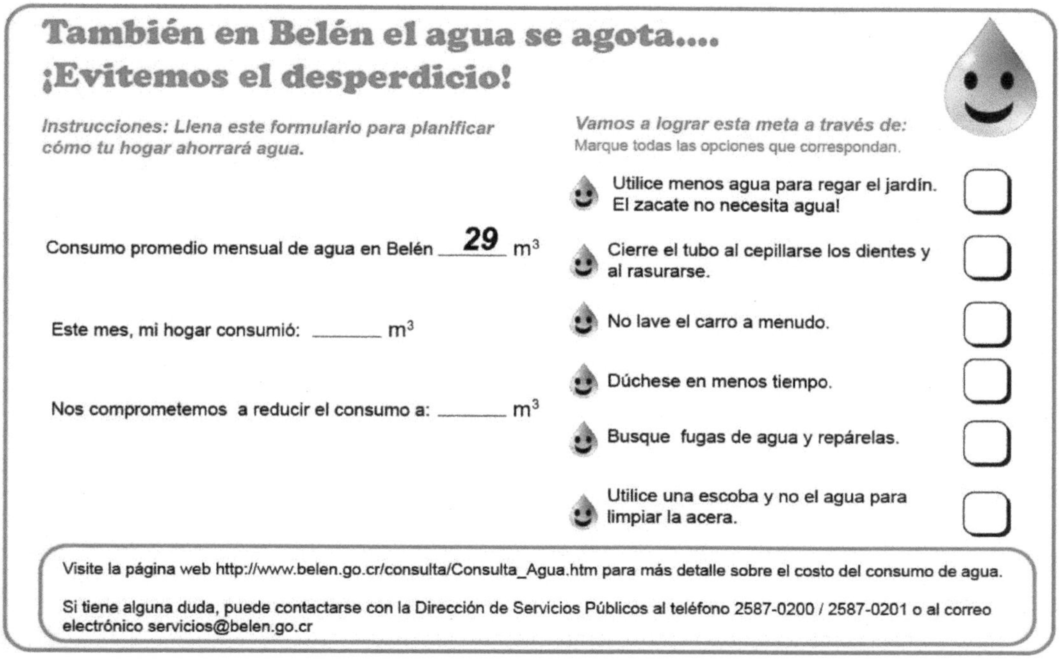

También en Belén el agua se agota....
¡Evitemos el desperdicio!

Instrucciones: Llena este formulario para planificar cómo tu hogar ahorrará agua.

Consumo promedio mensual de agua en Belén ___**29**___ m³

Este mes, mi hogar consumió: _____ m³

Nos comprometemos a reducir el consumo a: _____ m³

Vamos a lograr esta meta a través de:
Marque todas las opciones que correspondan.

- Utilice menos agua para regar el jardín. El zacate no necesita agua! ☐
- Cierre el tubo al cepillarse los dientes y al rasurarse. ☐
- No lave el carro a menudo. ☐
- Dúchese en menos tiempo. ☐
- Busque fugas de agua y repárelas. ☐
- Utilice una escoba y no el agua para limpiar la acera. ☐

Visite la página web http://www.belen.go.cr/consulta/Consulta_Agua.htm para más detalle sobre el costo del consumo de agua.

Si tiene alguna duda, puede contactarse con la Dirección de Servicios Públicos al teléfono 2587-0200 / 2587-0201 o al correo electrónico servicios@belen.go.cr

Source: © World Bank. Permission required for reuse.
Note: Worksheet says, "Water is scarce even in Belén. . . . Avoid waste! Instructions: Fill out this form to plan how you will save water. Average monthly water consumption in Belén 29 m³. This month, my house consumed: ___ m³. We are committed to reducing consumption to: ___ m³. We will achieve this goal through (check all options that apply): Use less water for the lawn; the lawn does not need water! Close the pipe while brushing teeth and shaving. Wash car less frequently. Take shorter showers. Look for water leaks and repair them. Use a broom and not the water to clean the sidewalk."

As table 1A.1 (in annex 1A) shows, there was no significant difference in baseline water consumption between the four randomized groups. Similarly, the data show no major difference between the groups in the two months before the intervention and the corresponding two months of the previous year.

Results

Result 1: Treatment Groups Reduce Water Consumption More Than Control Group (Difference-in-Differences)

Separated out by treatment status, table 1A.2 (annex 1A) demonstrates the differences between average water consumption in the postintervention period (August and September 2014) and in the 2013 rainy season.[5] The results reveal that average water consumption declined in all three treatment-group households more than in control households. However, the difference-in-differences is significant only for the neighborhood comparison and plan-making interventions (figure 1.5).

Figure 1.5 Change in Average Water Consumption, by Treatment Group, in Belén, Costa Rica

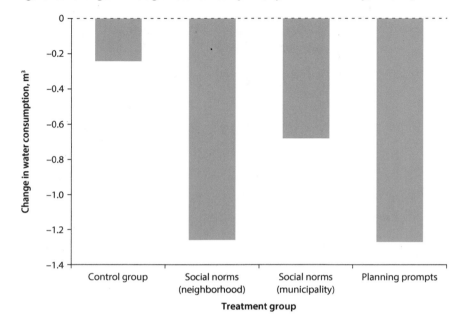

a. In the "social norms (neighborhood)" treatment, households were informed about how their water consumption compared with that of the average household in their neighborhood.
b. In the "social norms (municipality)" treatment, households were informed about how their water consumption compared with that of the average household in the city of Belén.
c. In the "planning prompts" treatment, households were informed about their consumption relative to the average Belén household and prompted to establish concrete steps to reduce it.

Result 2: Neighborhood Comparison Reduces Water Use Significantly, but City Comparison Has No Significant Effect

Table 1A.3 (annex 1A) presents our central regression results. We regress post-intervention water consumption on treatment status and control for baseline water consumption using four specifications of the baseline. The results across the first row show that, relative to the control group, the neighborhood comparison treatment reduces water consumption by between 0.98 and 1.47 cubic meters per household, or between 3.7 percent and 5.6 percent of water consumption for the control group over the same period. In contrast, there is no evidence that the city comparison reduced water consumption significantly in any specification. This accords with the literature, which indicates that localized norms are more effective at spurring behavior change than generalized norms with which people struggle to connect personally.

Result 3: Plan Making Reduces Water Use Significantly Relative to the Control Group

The results across the third row of table 1A.3 show that, relative to the control group, the plan-making treatment reduces water consumption by between 0.90 and 1.46 cubic meters per household, or between 3.4 percent and 5.5 percent of water consumption for the control group over the same period.[6]

Result 4: Pooled Data Confirm Effectiveness of Neighborhood Comparison and Plan-Making Interventions

Table 1A.4 pools the data for the months of August–September 2013 and August–September 2014, giving us two postintervention and two preintervention observations on each household in the sample. The point estimates suggest an effect size of around 4–5 percent of monthly water consumption for both interventions.

Based on the monthly average water consumption and the current water rates, our findings suggest that these two interventions resulted in estimated water savings worth C 1.4 million (US$2,600) to C 2.8 million (US$5,200). The cost of implementation amounted to around US$400, suggesting a benefit/cost ratio varying from 6.5 to 13. This justifies the intervention's expansion to the entire municipality.

The results indicate that approximately 6,720 cubic meters of water could be preserved in Belén each month. This is equivalent to 87,300 baths and is enough to forestall the advent of substantial short-term water shortages in the municipality.

Result 5: Plan-Making and Neighborhood Comparison Interventions Appear Most Effective for Low-Consumption and High-Consumption Households, Respectively

Finally, table 1A.5 (annex 1A) presents an analysis of potential heterogeneous effects across subgroups, based on dividing each group by its initial consumption during the May–November 2013 rainy season. This information helps us to target responsive subgroups more cost-effectively and to avoid wasting money (and political capital) on nonresponsive subgroups (Ferraro and Miranda 2013).

The results in columns I–III show that the neighborhood comparison intervention for the above median-consumption households nearly doubles the average effect for the whole city. The plan-making treatment, meanwhile, is relatively more effective when applied to households with below-median consumption. This suggests that policy makers may benefit from targeting interventions to specific household subsets.

Columns IV–VIII, which further divide households by quintiles, demonstrate that households with initially high consumption reveal the largest effects (although the effect sizes are not statistically significant). The lowest quintile of households sees the second largest decrease in consumption, on the other hand, with such households responding most strongly to the plan-making intervention.

The heterogeneous effects across households show some interesting (but weak) patterns. Among the possible explanations here is that members of households with low initial consumption may already be motivated to save water (possibly owing to higher financial constraints). They are therefore predisposed to translate these intentions into concrete actions, as prompted by the plan-making intervention. In contrast, households with high initial consumption may have responded positively to the neighborhood comparison intervention because it highlighted information hitherto unknown to them (that is, how much water they are currently using overall, or how their current consumption levels compare with their neighbors).

To summarize our results, we find that informing individuals about how their behaviors compared with those of their peers has measurable effects on water consumption, and that comparisons with more-proximate peer groups are more effective. We also find that prompting people to set their own goals for water conservation, and to make plans to realize these goals, reduces their water use similarly. Both interventions attain comparable results, although they are driven by distinctive consumer subgroups.

Conclusion

This study is perhaps the first to apply behavioral economics to water use in a low- or middle-income country, and to do so at a subnational government level.

The significance of these findings partly derives from the growing urgency of reducing water consumption in LMICs given rising levels of water stress. The positive results of the pilots suggest that governments should consider using behavior-based interventions to supplement current price- and persuasion-based tools. This pilot project should give confidence to municipal governments in LMICs that such interventions can be implemented without the need for considerable resources or advanced technologies.

Strengthening the capacity of local governments to raise resources and finance the provision of public services to their residents effectively is a key issue in development. In this respect, we believe it is important to look beyond the immediate context of water use in Costa Rica and consider how the pilot might contribute to the study of urban governance and government capacity in LMICs globally.

Annex 1A Supplementary Tables

Table 1A.1 Baseline Water Consumption Measures in Belén, Costa Rica, Randomization Check

Water consumption (m³)	Control	Neighborhood comparison[a]		Municipality comparison[b]		Planning postcard[c]	
		Treatment	Difference (C-T)	Treatment	Difference (C-T)	Treatment	Difference (C-T)
Average monthly consumption, December 2012–November 2013 (m³)	27.38	27.47	−0.09	27.21	0.17	27.85	−0.47
(SE)	(0.58)	(0.69)	(0.90)	(0.50)	(0.77)	(0.65)	(0.87)
No. of households	1,312	1,287	2,599	1,287	2,599	1,274	2,586
Average monthly consumption, January–November 2013 (m³)	25.59	25.58	0.02	25.39	0.20	26.01	−0.42
(SE)	(0.54)	(0.64)	(0.84)	(0.47)	(0.72)	(0.61)	(0.81)

table continues next page

Table 1A.1 Baseline Water Consumption Measures in Belén, Costa Rica, Randomization Check *(continued)*

Water consumption (m³)	Control	Neighborhood comparison[a]		Municipality comparison[b]		Planning postcard[c]	
		Treatment	Difference (C-T)	Treatment	Difference (C-T)	Treatment	Difference (C-T)
No. of households	1,312	1,287	2,599	1,287	2,599	1,274	2,586
Average monthly consumption, May–November 2013 (m³)	28.07	28.02	0.05	27.80	0.27	29.09	−1.02
(SE)	(0.60)	(0.76)	(0.97)	(0.58)	(0.84)	(0.71)	(0.93)
No. of households	1,339	1,321	2,660	1,309	2,648	1,304	2,643
Year-over-year increase in consumption, May/June 2012–May/June 2013 (m³)	1.25	1.42	−0.16	1.33	−0.07	1.24	0.01
(SE)	(0.06)	(0.11)	(0.13)	(0.09)	(0.10)	(0.10)	(0.11)
No. of households	1,324	1,299	2,623	1,293	2,617	1,282	2,606

Note: Numbers in parentheses are standard errors (SE). Differences between treated and control groups are not statistically significant.
C-T = difference between control and treatment groups; m³ = cubic meters.
a. The "neighborhood comparison" treatment used a descriptive norm approach, whereby the treatment households were informed about how their water consumption compared with that of the average household in their neighborhood.
b. The "municipality comparison" treatment used a descriptive norm approach, whereby the treatment households were informed about how their water consumption compared with that of the average household in the city of Belén.
c. The "planning postcard" treatment used a plan-making approach, whereby the treatment households were informed about their consumption relative to the average Belén household and prompted to establish concrete steps to reduce it.

Table 1A.2 Difference-in-Differences in Water Consumption, Belén, Costa Rica

Treatment and measurement type	ΔControl	ΔTreatment	ΔT–ΔC
Treatment 1: Neighborhood comparison[a]			
Difference between average monthly post-treatment consumption (August–September 2014) and average monthly consumption in pretreatment rainy season (May–November 2013) (m³)	−0.24	−1.50	−1.26*
(SE)	(0.40)	(0.53)	(0.66)
No. of households	1,285	1,267	2,552
Treatment 2: Municipality comparison[b]			
Difference between average monthly post-treatment consumption (August–September 2014) and average monthly consumption in pretreatment rainy season (May–November 2013) (m³)	−0.24	−0.93	−0.68
(SE)	(0.40)	(0.44)	(0.60)
No. of households	1,285	1,261	2,546
Treatment 3: Planning postcard[c]			
Difference between average monthly post-treatment consumption (August–September 2014) and average monthly consumption in pretreatment rainy season (May–November 2013)	−0.24	−1.52	−1.27**
(SE)	(0.40)	(0.43)	(0.59)
No. of households	1,285	1,248	2,533

Note: Numbers in parentheses are standard errors (SE). T = treatment; C = control; m³ = cubic meters.
a. The "neighborhood comparison" treatment used a descriptive norm approach, whereby the treatment households were informed about how their water consumption compared with that of the average household in their neighborhood.
b. The "municipality comparison" treatment used a descriptive norm approach, whereby the treatment households were informed about how their water consumption compared with that of the average household in the city of Belén.
c. The "planning postcard" treatment used a plan-making approach, whereby the treatment households were informed about their consumption relative to the average Belén household and prompted to establish concrete steps to reduce it.
*$p < 0.10$; **$p < 0.05$.

Table 1A.3 Effect of Treatments on Average Post-Treatment Water Consumption in Belén, Costa Rica

Outcome variable: Average of August and September 2014 water consumption (m³)	(I)	(II)	(III)	(IV)	(V)	(VI)	(VII)	(VIII)
Treatment 1: Neighborhood comparison								
(m³)[a]	−1.27*	−1.28**	−0.98**	−1.47**	−1.27*	−1.29**	−0.99**	−1.47**
(SE)	(0.67)	(0.60)	(0.50)	(0.58)	(0.67)	(0.60)	(0.49)	(0.58)
Treatment 2: Municipality comparison								
(m³)[b]	−0.81	−0.81	−0.77	−0.92	−0.82	−0.83	−0.77	−0.92
(SE)	(0.65)	(0.58)	(0.50)	(0.56)	(0.65)	(0.58)	(0.49)	(0.56)
Treatment 3: Planning postcard								
(m³)[c]	−1.11*	−1.23**	−0.90**	−1.46***	−1.13*	−1.26**	−0.93**	−1.49***
(SE)	(0.64)	(0.59)	(0.46)	(0.57)	(0.64)	(0.59)	(0.46)	(0.57)
Constant	11.40***	7.12***	2.96***	6.09***	8.77***	5.41***	1.42	4.97***
(SE)	(2.13)	(1.89)	(1.12)	(1.71)	(1.97)	(1.75)	(1.25)	(1.59)
August and September 2013 total consumption	Yes	No	No	No	Yes	No	No	No
Rainy season 2013 total consumption (May–November 2013) (m³)	No	Yes	Yes	No	No	Yes	Yes	No
May–June 2014 total consumption (m³)	No	No	Yes	No	No	No	Yes	No
Average annual consumption (December 2012–November 2013) (m³)	No	No	No	Yes	No	No	No	Yes
Fixed effects for billing date	No	No	No	No	Yes	Yes	Yes	Yes
Observations	5,126	5,061	5,061	5,061	5,126	5,061	5,061	5,061
R-squared	0.41	0.52	0.68	0.56	0.41	0.53	0.69	0.56

Note: Numbers in parentheses are standard errors (SE). m³ = cubic meters.

a. The "neighborhood comparison" treatment used a descriptive norm approach, whereby the treatment households were informed about how their water consumption compared with that of the average household in their neighborhood.

b. The "municipality comparison" treatment used a descriptive norm approach, whereby the treatment households were informed about how their water consumption compared with that of the average household in the city of Belén.

c. The "planning postcard" treatment used a plan-making approach, whereby the treatment households were informed about their consumption relative to the average Belén household and prompted to establish concrete steps to reduce it.

*p < 0.10; **p < 0.05; ***p < 0.01.

Table 1A.4 Effect of Treatments on Water Consumption, Repeated Household Observations, in Belén, Costa Rica

Outcome variable: Average of August and September 2013 and 2014 water consumption (m³)	(I)	(II)
2014 consumption dummy	−0.13	−0.13
(SE)	(0.45)	(0.45)
Treatment 1: Neighborhood comparison[a]	0.10	0.10
(SE)	(0.98)	(0.98)
Treatment 2: Municipality comparison[b]	−0.20	−0.20
(SE)	(0.83)	(0.83)
Treatment 3: Planning postcard[c]	0.21	0.21
(SE)	(0.93)	(0.93)
2014 consumption dummy x treatment 1	−1.34*	−1.35*
(SE)	(0.81)	(0.81)
2014 consumption dummy x treatment 2	−0.97	−0.97
(SE)	(0.70)	(0.70)

table continues next page

Table 1A.4 Effect of Treatments on Water Consumption, Repeated Household Observations, in Belén, Costa Rica *(continued)*

Outcome variable: Average of August and September 2013 and 2014 water consumption (m³)	(I)	(II)
2014 consumption dummy x treatment 3	−1.28*	−1.28*
(SE)	(0.67)	(0.67)
Constant	26.54***	26.67***
(SE)	(0.57)	(0.58)
Monthly fixed effects	No	Yes
Observations	20,939	20,939
R-squared	0.00	0.00

Note: Numbers in parentheses are standard errors (SE). m³ = cubic meters.

a. The "neighborhood comparison" treatment used a descriptive norm approach, whereby the treatment households were informed about how their water consumption compared with that of the average household in their neighborhood.

b. The "municipality comparison" treatment used a descriptive norm approach, whereby the treatment households were informed about how their water consumption compared with that of the average household in the city of Belén.

c. The "planning postcard" treatment used a plan-making approach, whereby the treatment households were informed about their consumption relative to the average Belén household and prompted to establish concrete steps to reduce it.

*$p < 0.10$; **$p < 0.05$; ***$p < 0.01$.

Table 1A.5 Effect of Treatments on Average Post-Treatment Water Consumption, by Subgroup, in Belén, Costa Rica

Outcome variable: Average of August and September 2014 water consumption (m³)	Full sample (I)	Below median consumption (II)	Above median consumption (III)	First quintile (IV)	Second quintile (V)	Third quintile (VI)	Fourth quintile (VII)	Fifth quintile (VIII)
Treatment 1: Neighborhood comparison	−1.28*	−0.38	−2.03**	−0.92	−0.46	−0.65	−0.80	−3.25
(SE)	(0.60)	(0.54)	(1.06)	(0.87)	(0.88)	(0.82)	(1.30)	(2.33)
Treatment 2: Municipality comparison	−0.81	−0.45	−1.15	−1.30	−0.31	0.14	0.14	−2.62
(SE)	(0.58)	(0.52)	(1.03)	(0.85)	(0.84)	(0.78)	(1.40)	(2.09)
Treatment 3: Planning postcard	−1.23*	−0.97**	−1.47	−1.53**	−1.23	−0.21	−1.22	−1.88
(SE)	(0.59)	(0.48)	(1.06)	(0.78)	(0.80)	(0.76)	(1.31)	(2.26)
Constant	7.12***	4.59***	10.73***	5.39***	3.51***	−0.21	6.80	12.42
(SE)	(1.89)	(0.59)	(4.61)	(0.94)	(2.19)	(3.04)	(5.28)	(8.75)
Observations	5,061	2,534	2,527	1,004	1,024	1,032	1,004	997
R-squared	0.52	0.24	0.40	0.10	0.04	0.06	0.03	0.37

Note: Numbers in parentheses are standard errors (SE). m³ = cubic meters.

a. The "neighborhood comparison" treatment used a descriptive norm approach, whereby the treatment households were informed about how their water consumption compared with that of the average household in their neighborhood.

b. The "municipality comparison" treatment used a descriptive norm approach, whereby the treatment households were informed about how their water consumption compared with that of the average household in the city of Belén.

c. The "planning postcard" treatment used a plan-making approach, whereby the treatment households were informed about their consumption relative to the average Belén household and prompted to establish concrete steps to reduce it.

*$p < 0.10$; **$p < 0.05$; ***$p < 0.01$.

Notes

1. Population data from the Costa Rica 2011 Census, National Institute of Statistics and Census, San José: http://www.inec.go.cr/.

2. We excluded commercial establishments and residential condominium associations, which receive a joint bill rather than household-level bills.

3. In June 2014, the Municipality of Belén started to change water meters. Because of the inability to merge post-experiment houses by their meter number, we lost approximately 8 percent of the original randomized sample. The numbers of observations dropped are homogeneous across treatment arms.

4. For simplicity in this volume and its tables, we refer to the water consumption on which the bill for month X is based as "Month X Billed Consumption."

5. By using the rainy season of 2013 as our measure of "pre-intervention" water consumption, we can minimize the seasonal factors that would occur if we were to use, for example, the two months immediately before the intervention.

6. As with the neighborhood comparison, the choice of baseline consumption measure affects the size of the coefficients but not their sign or significance: they are consistently negative and statistically significant.

References

Aguilar, C. 2014. "Context of Integrated Urban Water Management in Desamparados, Costa Rica." Unpublished manuscript, World Bank, Washington, DC.

Bower, Kathleen. 2014. "Water Supply and Sanitation of Costa Rica." *Environmental Earth Sciences* 71 (1): 107–23

Chetty, R., A. Looney, and K. Kroft. 2009. "Salience and Taxation: Theory and Evidence." *American Economic Review* 99 (4): 1145–77.

Datta, S., and S. Mullainathan. 2014. "Behavioral Design for Development." *Review of Income and Wealth* 60 (1): 7–35.

El Tiempo. 2014. "Seis embalses están en la peor crisis en cinco años: Municipios de Cundinamarca se enfrentan a racionamiento de agua" [Six reservoirs are in the worst crisis in five years: municipalities of Cundinamarca face water rationing]. *El Tiempo*, May 15.

Ferraro, P. J., and J. J. Miranda. 2013. "Heterogeneous Treatment Effects and Mechanisms in Information-Based Environmental Policies: Evidence from a Large-Scale Field Experiment." *Resource and Energy Economics* 35 (3): 356–79.

Ferraro, P. J., and M. K. Price. 2013. "Using Nonpecuniary Strategies to Influence Behavior: Evidence from a Large-Scale Field Experiment." *Review of Economics and Statistics* 95 (1): 64–73.

Foster, V. 2005. "Ten Years of Water Service Reform in Latin America: Toward an Anglo-French Model." Water Supply and Sanitation Sector Board Discussion Paper No. 3, World Bank, Washington, DC.

Goldstein, Noah J., Robert B. Cialdini, and Vladas Griskevicius. 2008. "A Room with a Viewpoint: Using Social Norms to Motivate Environmental Conservation in Hotels." *Journal of Consumer Research* 35 (3): 472–82.

Municipality of Belén. 2010. "Plan Maestro de los Sistemas de Abastecimiento de Agua Potable de Belén de Heredia" [Master Plan for Potable Water Supply Systems of Belén of Heredia]. Planning document, Municipality of Belén, Costa Rica.

Olmstead, S. M., W. M. Hanemann, and R. N. Stavins. 2007. "Water Demand under Alternative Price Structures." NBER Working Paper 13573, National Bureau of Economic Research, Cambridge, MA.

Rogers, Todd, Katy Milkman, Leslie John, and Michael I. Norton. 2013. "Making the Best-Laid Plans Better: How Plan Making Increases Follow-Through." Working paper, Harvard University, Cambridge, MA.

Scanzerla, T. 2014. "São Paulo Is Running Out of Water, but Authorities Say There's No Need for Rationing." *Global Voices Online*, October 17.

UNDP (United Nations Development Programme). 2006. *Human Development Report 2006—Beyond Scarcity: Power, Poverty and the Global Water Crisis*. New York: Palgrave Macmillan.

CHAPTER 2

Promoting Tax Compliance in Guatemala Using Behavioral Economics: Evidence from Two Randomized Trials

Stewart Kettle, Marco Antonio Hernández Oré, Simon Ruda, and Michael Sanders

Introduction

Improving tax compliance is a major policy priority in Guatemala. Between 2011 and 2015 total government revenues in Guatemala amounted to about 12 percent of gross domestic product (GDP), less than half the Latin American average of 26 percent. Despite its status as a middle-income country, Guatemala languishes near the bottom of the International Monetary Fund's World Economic Outlook measure of revenue-to-GDP ratio. Unlike other countries that collect significant nontax revenues (for example, from natural resources), the Guatemalan government relies on tax revenues for 90 percent of its income (World Bank 2014).

Partly because of these low rates of revenue collection, the Guatemalan authorities have limited fiscal and administrative resources, which constrain their ability to implement complex changes to the tax system. Moreover, because of political opposition and bureaucratic inertia, policy makers have historically struggled to approve and implement tax reforms (World Bank 2014). In this context, nonregulatory interventions rooted in the experimental methodology of behavioral economics can provide a valuable alternative to more conventional reform programs (Slemrod and Weber 2012).

The behavioral economics literature presents a range of possibilities for enhancing tax compliance. These include simple reminders to taxpayers, deterrent

---

This chapter is partially based on the following two papers: Kettle, S., M. Hernandez, S. Ruda, and M. Sanders. 2016. "Behavioral Interventions in Tax Compliance: Evidence from Guatemala." Policy Research Working Paper 7690, World Bank, Washington, DC; and Kettle, S., M. Hernandez, O. Hauser, S. Ruda, and M. Sanders. 2017. "Failure to CAPTCHA Attention: Null Results from an Honesty Priming Experiment in Guatemala." *Behavioral Sciences* 7 (2): 28.

messages underscoring the legal obligation to pay taxes, and appeals to social norms or to a sense of moral duty. Recent experiments suggest that interventions that increase the perceived probability of enforcement actions or the perceived severity of sanctions are the most effective in boosting taxpayer compliance (Hallsworth 2014). However, the magnitude of the effects recorded in these studies is influenced by local contextual factors.

Only a handful of randomized control trials (RCTs) on tax behavior have been carried out in low- and middle-income countries (LMICs), including in Latin America, and their results have been mixed. For example, an experiment conducted in three Lima, Peru, municipalities showed that sending taxpayers a simple reminder message and a social norms message, both in the form of a physical letter, were effective in increasing tax compliance, while a deterrence message was ineffective (Del Carpio 2013). However, a similar trial in the Junín municipality of Buenos Aires, Argentina, revealed the precise opposite: only a deterrence message was effective, while reminder and social norms messages had no impact on taxpayer behavior (Castro and Scartascini 2013). These inconsistencies likely result from both contextual specifics (such as differences in national tax regimes, levels of public trust in institutions, local social norms, and tax culture) and experimental design factors (such as variations in how the messages were presented or specific taxpayer groups were targeted).

Two recent RCT experiments implemented by the Guatemalan Tax Authority (Superintendencia de Administración Tributaria, or SAT) have yielded important insights into tax compliance. Unlike similar trials in other countries, one of these RCTs showed a significant impact on tax compliance that endured over the medium term. Moreover, the low cost of the experiment and its potential to increase fiscal revenue have underscored the enormous value for money that behavioral interventions can generate.

The behavioral messages in the second RCT did not produce significant results, but these robust null results help to direct policy makers in Guatemala away from interventions that are unlikely to be effective. Although these experiments were designed and independently evaluated by a team of international researchers, their modest financial and administrative costs illustrate the relative ease with which LMIC governments can carry out sophisticated behavioral testing and formulate interventions that are demonstrably effective in the local context.

Experiment 1: Reminder Letters to Promote Tax Compliance

Behavioral Messages in Reminder Letters

In 2015 a small team of researchers working together with SAT launched an RCT experiment designed to test whether sending reminder letters to taxpayers could influence income tax compliance and, if so, to determine which of the different messages included in the letters were most effective (Kettle et al. 2016). This experiment was similar to recent trials in Peru and Argentina, which, as noted above, had produced conflicting results. Yet, this experiment broadened the scope of the intervention to include firms as well as individual taxpayers, and it covered the entire country.

Both firms and individuals received one of five messages from SAT in the form of a physical letter delivered to a registered postal address. These messages were framed in five different ways that reflect five different theories of tax compliance. Table 2.1 summarizes the content of each letter, and the subsequent text describes in greater detail the behavioral insights used in each one.

The first letter—the original SAT letter—was used to test the impact of a simple reminder message. The letter emphasized the upcoming tax deadline but did not inform the recipient about how to declare his or her tax liability. The letter also did not highlight that failing to declare would entail any legal, social, or moral consequences.

The research team developed four additional treatment letters designed to test various messages. The simplest of these was known as the "behavioral design" letter, because it incorporated several features designed to bolster compliance. The letter drew on deterrence messaging, informing the recipient that declaring income tax was mandatory and that a failure to comply could result in legal sanctions. The letter began with a short "call to action" designed to catch the

Table 2.1 Treatment Groups and Messages in Letter Experiment to Promote Tax Compliance in Guatemala, 2015

Group	Description
Control group	• No letter
Original tax authority letter (reminder message)	• Simple reminder to declare, no information on how to declare
Behavioral design letter	• Began with short "call to action" that declaration is needed now • Specified where to declare (website address) • Informed taxpayers they can pay in installments • Included deterrent message: *"If you do not declare, you may be audited and face the procedure established by law."*
Behavioral design + social norm letter	• Like behavioral design letter but included social norm message: *"According to our records, 64.5 percent of Guatemalans declared their income tax for the year 2013 on time. You are part of the minority of Guatemalans who are yet to declare for this tax."*
Behavioral design + deliberate choice letter	• Like behavioral design letter but included deliberate choice message: *"Previously we have considered your failure to declare an oversight. However, if you don't declare now, we will consider it an active choice and you may therefore be audited and could face the procedure established by law."*
Behavioral design + national pride letter	• Like behavioral design letter but excluded call to action and deterrent message • Softer tone, including image of Guatemalan flag and the phrase: *"You are a Guatemalan citizen and Guatemala needs you. Be a good citizen and submit the 2013 annual return of income tax … Are you going to support your country?"*

Source: Kettle et al. 2016.

recipient's attention ("Please file your declaration of income tax"); it noted that payments can be made in installments;[1] and it directed the recipient to the tax authority website.[2] The letter was also rewritten with simple and clear language, eliminating nonessential text from the original letter.

The other three letters used the same template as the behavioral design letter. The only difference was the inclusion of an additional message at the beginning of the letter. The "social norms" message was rooted in the notion that expectations regarding the behavior of peers largely determine taxpayer compliance (Kirchler 2007; Torgler 2007). It noted that most Guatemalans (64.5 percent)[3] had declared their income taxes on time and stated that the recipient was now in a noncompliant minority. The message attempted to leverage the desire to comply with social norms by emphasizing the social normalcy of tax compliance and the implicitly aberrant or antisocial nature of tax evasion. Although the "social norms" letter made no explicit reference to enforcement, it clearly implied that the authorities were aware of the recipient's failure to declare tax liability.

The "deliberate choice" letter made it clear that the authorities would regard noncompliance as an intentional decision. The message was based on the idea that tax evasion primarily results from force of habit in a context of lax oversight (Anderson 2003). The letter addressed the recipient's tendency to continue doing whatever has been successful in the past, known as "status quo bias," by presenting the failure to file taxes as a deliberate choice for which the individual is morally and legally culpable. The message also stated that the recipient's actions were being monitored.

Finally, the "national pride" letter presented taxpaying as a patriotic responsibility. It encouraged the recipient to "be a good citizen" and support their country by paying income taxes. It also incorporated an image of the Guatemalan flag. The letter included no references to enforcement in order to better isolate the patriotic motivation (Sheffrin and Triest 1992).

Letter Experiment Context and Design

Guatemala's tax system includes two income tax regimes: the default option is a gross income tax, and the alternative is a profit tax. The gross income tax is calculated as a simple percentage of earned income, whereas the profit tax involves a number of exemptions and deductions. Individuals and firms must decide which tax to pay at the beginning of each tax year. Taxpayers in the gross income tax regime must calculate their returns monthly, while profit tax returns must be calculated every three months. The trial focused on the profit tax for four main reasons:

- Its quarterly schedule allows for a clearer distinction between timely compliance and delinquency.
- The more-complex calculations involved in filing the profit tax make the amounts reported sensitive to both the honesty and the fastidiousness of the taxpayer.

- The accounting requirements of the profit tax make it more closely comparable to the income tax regimes of other countries.[4]
- The profit tax includes the proceeds from unincorporated small businesses as well as income earned by self-employed professionals, allowing the research team to evaluate the effect of different interventions on both firms and individuals.

The research team developed an anonymized sample based on official data. SAT had identified 115,999 taxpayers due to declare their annual profit tax for the 2013 fiscal year, and isolated 44,952 who had failed to do so by May 16, 2014. Of these 44,952 taxpayers, the research team excluded 1,565 taxpayers whom SAT had already contacted.

The remaining 43,387 taxpayers were randomly assigned to one of six trial groups: a control group of 12,397 taxpayers and five treatment groups of between 6,197 and 6,199 taxpayers each. Randomization was conducted at the individual level with no stratification.[5] The five treatment groups were sent one of the five letters detailed above.

The research team estimated the impact of the letters on the rate of declaration as well as the total amount paid by the taxpayers, estimated in local currency. The impact of the letters was calculated 11 weeks after the messages were sent out.

Letter Experiment Results

All of the letters significantly boosted income tax declarations, including the original reminder letter already used by the tax authority (figure 2.1). However, while the experiment provided an important validation of the government's current approach, it also revealed several superior strategies.

Overall, the "social norms" and "deliberate choice" letters proved to be the most effective. The "deliberate choice" letter increased declarations by 5.4 percentage points (or 46 percent) over the control group and by 1.8 percentage points (or 10 percent) over the original reminder letter. Moreover, it was the only letter that performed statistically significantly better than the original reminder letter in terms of increasing declarations.

The impacts of the behavioral letters on the average amounts paid were more pronounced (figure 2.2). Again, the "social norms" and "deliberate choice" letters were the most effective, increasing the average payment amounts per taxpayer by 1.7 and 1.4 percentage points, respectively. In addition, the average amount paid by letter recipients who reported positive tax liability also rose by 43.6 percent and 38.5 percent, respectively. While taxpayers in the control group paid an average of US$6.70, this figure more than doubled among those who received the "social norms" letter (US$13.90) and nearly tripled among recipients of the "deliberate choice" letter (US$18.00). Meanwhile, the original SAT letter failed to increase the average amount paid.

The project also revealed that the "social norms" and "deliberate choice" letters were especially effective in promoting tax compliance among firms. Firms that

Figure 2.1 Shares of Guatemalan Taxpayers Declaring Taxes in Response to Experimental Messages, by Treatment Type, 2015

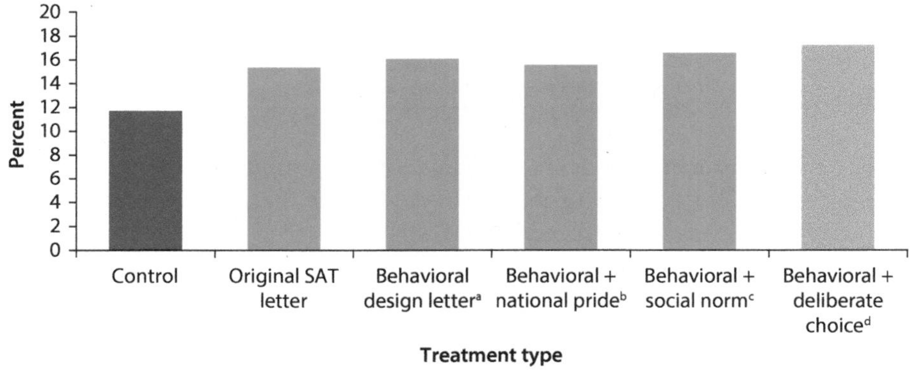

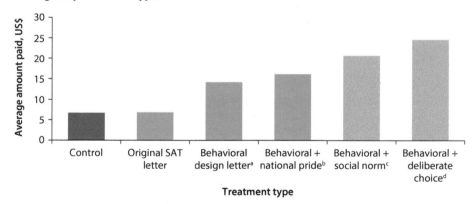

Source: Kettle et al. 2016.

Note: Figure shows response levels 11 weeks after letters were sent to treatment groups. The control group received no letter. Green bar denotes point estimates significantly different from the original Guatemalan Tax Authority (SAT) letter at the 1 percent level of significance.

a. The "behavioral design" letter included a deterrent "nudge" message focusing on the cost of noncompliance: possible auditing and legal proceedings.

b. The "behavioral + national pride" letter included a softer "nudge" message to be "a good citizen," with a "call to action" focusing on the national responsibility of paying taxes.

c. The "behavioral + social norm" letter included a deterrent "nudge" message emphasizing that most Guatemalans declare their taxes on time.

d. The "behavioral + deliberate choice" letter included a deterrent "nudge" message framing failure to declare and pay as intentional dishonesty.

Figure 2.2 Average Amount Paid by Guatemalan Taxpayers Receiving Experimental Messages, by Treatment Type, 2015

Source: Kettle et al. 2016.

Note: Figure shows amounts paid 11 weeks after letters were sent to treatment groups. The control group received no letter. Green bars denote point estimates significantly different from the original Guatemalan Tax Authority (SAT) letter at the 1 percent level of significance.

a. The "behavioral design" letter included a deterrent "nudge" message focusing on the cost of noncompliance: possible auditing and legal proceedings.

b. The "behavioral + national pride" letter included a softer "nudge" message to be "a good citizen," with a "call to action" focusing on the national responsibility of paying taxes.

c. The "behavioral + social norm" letter included a deterrent "nudge" message emphasizing that most Guatemalans declare their taxes on time.

d. The "behavioral + deliberate choice" letter included a deterrent "nudge" message framing failure to declare and pay as intentional dishonesty.

received these letters made average tax payments of US$27.60 and US$37.10, respectively—far larger than the control group average of US$6.70.

Among the most striking features of this trial was its high benefit-cost ratio. The cost of the experiment was modest. Sending the letters to all participants cost just US$15,065. In addition, SAT conducted the project in less than three weeks using existing systems, processes, and personnel. By contrast, the benefits of the experiment were large. The "deliberate choice" letter was the most effective in improving both income tax declaration rates and payment amounts. Had this letter been sent to the entire sample group, it would have generated an estimated US$757,837 *more* than the cost of the project, representing a staggering 36-fold return on investment. Even including the less-effective letters, the project boosted actual net tax revenue by US$288,301.

Further data were collected 12 months after the trial for the research team to determine whether the letters had caused any habituation in tax payment (with no further reminders). The results show that the taxpayers who had received the "social norms" or "deliberate choice" letters declared significantly more than those in the other groups the following tax year. Those two letters each boosted the 2016 rate of payment by an estimated 0.7 percentage points, an increase of 16 percent over the control group (figure 2.3). These results indicate that compliance rates may remain elevated in the future without the need for further interventions and that the initial increase in tax compliance may be reinforced by habit.

Figure 2.3 Shares of Guatemalan Taxpayers Who Paid Taxes One Year after Experiment (in 2016), with No Further Reminder

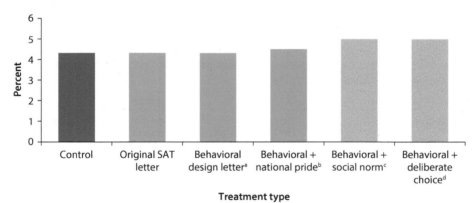

Source: Kettle et al. 2016.
Note: Figure shows amounts paid 11 weeks after letters were sent to treatment groups. The control group received no letter. Green bars denote point estimates significantly different from the original Guatemalan Tax Authority (SAT) letter at the 1 percent level of significance.
a. The "behavioral design" letter included a deterrent "nudge" message focusing on the cost of noncompliance: possible auditing and legal proceedings.
b. The "behavioral + national pride" letter included a softer "nudge" message to be "a good citizen," with a "call to action" focusing on the national responsibility of paying taxes.
c. The "behavioral + social norm" letter included a deterrent "nudge" message emphasizing that most Guatemalans declare their taxes on time.
d. The "behavioral + deliberate choice" letter included a deterrent "nudge" message framing failure to declare and pay as intentional dishonesty.

Experiment 2: Online CAPTCHA Prompts to Improve Accuracy of Tax Declarations

Trials similar to Experiment 1 in other countries (Hallsworth 2014) have yielded a wealth of information on the relative effectiveness of different messages in different contexts. However, sending physical letters to taxpayers is only one of many prospective strategies for improving tax compliance using behavioral economics. Technological innovations present new possibilities for influencing taxpayer behavior, and in the future physical letters delivered by mail may no longer be (if they have ever been) the most effective method for a given country.

Behavioral Messages in CAPTCHA Online Experiment

A second trial in Guatemala demonstrates the possibilities presented by an expanding technological frontier (Kettle et al. 2017). In this case, the research team attempted to leverage Guatemala's online tax declaration system to improve the accuracy of income tax reporting. The team developed a series of CAPTCHA prompts,[6] which appeared on the screen just before the taxpayer entered SAT's online tax filing system, Declaraguate.[7] These prompts were inserted into the CAPTCHA response that taxpayers had to complete before presenting their declarations.

The experiment tested six different short messages related to honesty and ethical behavior, three of which were framed in the form of a question (table 2.2). The purpose of these messages was to bring ethical, legal, and moral issues to the taxpayer's attention and thereby encourage more honest reporting.

The first message (the "honesty declaration" in table 2.2) prompted users to verify that they were filing their tax declaration honestly, following Shu et al. (2012). The second message ("public good") noted that taxes helped

Table 2.2 Experiment Treatment Groups and Messages in CAPTCHA Experiment to Promote Tax Compliance in Guatemala, 2014–15

Group	Description
Control group	• Typical CAPTCHA website design. Box states, "Please type the characters that you see in the picture." • Once the characters from the picture are typed, the taxpayer can click on the "fill form" button to access the declaration form.
Honesty declaration	• Includes an honesty declaration: "I will fill out this form honestly, please sign your name to confirm this declaration." • The taxpayer must then enter their name in a box below this statement before being able to press the "fill form" button.
Public good	• Includes an image of the Guatemalan flag and the following public good message: "In 2013 your taxes helped pay for schools, hospitals, and policemen."
Enforcement	• Includes an image of a gavel and the following message: "5,060 taxpayers in early 2014 had legal proceedings for breach of their tax obligations."

table continues next page

Table 2.2 Experiment Treatment Groups and Messages in CAPTCHA Experiment to Promote Tax Compliance in Guatemala, 2014–15 *(continued)*

Group	Description
Choice of public good	• Gives the taxpayer a choice of public goods on which to spend their tax payment: "Please choose what you want us to direct your tax money to." • The taxpayer must choose one of the options—schools, hospitals, or police—before they can press the "fill form" button.
Choice of enforcement	• Gives the taxpayer a choice of the punishment that people should receive for fraudulent tax declaration: "Please tell us what you think should happen to people who fill out their forms dishonestly." • The taxpayer must choose one of the options—pay a fine, have assets confiscated, or go to jail—before they can press the "fill form" button.
Self-select "I am honest"	• Allows the taxpayer to self-select into being honest, asking "Which of the following do you identify with?" • The taxpayer must select one of two options—"I am an honest taxpayer who declares truthfully" or "I'm a busy taxpayer who declares quickly"—before they can press the "fill form" button.

Source: Kettle et al. 2017.

finance vital public goods such as schools and hospitals. The third message ("enforcement") focused on deterrence by noting the number of taxpayers who had been prosecuted for tax-related offenses in the previous year. The fourth message ("choice of public good") reframed the public goods motivation as a choice, asking taxpayers which types of public goods they would like their taxes to finance, based on a prior finding that even the illusion of choice of public spending increases tax compliance (Lamberton, De Neve, and Norton 2014). The fifth message ("choice of enforcement") revisited the deterrence motivation by asking taxpayers to determine what punishment should be applied to tax evaders. The sixth message ("self-select 'I am honest'") asked respondents to describe themselves as either honest taxpayers who were filing accurate declarations or busy taxpayers who were filing in a hurry.

Distinctive Features of CAPTCHA Experiment Design

The CAPTCHA experiment differed from the letter experiment in several important respects:

• It exclusively targeted taxpayers who were already in the process of filing their declarations, whereas the letter experiment exclusively targeted delinquent filers.
• It focused entirely on the accuracy of those declarations, expressed in terms of the amount of taxes declared, whereas the letter experiment primarily attempted to influence the subject's decision to declare income tax liability.

- The control group did complete a CAPTCHA prompt, albeit one that contained no substantive message, whereas the control group in the letter experiment received no letter.
- It involved a much larger sample group than the letter experiment, encompassing 715,190 taxpayers across the country and 3,232,430 tax declarations made over a period of four months. The sample group went beyond the income tax and targeted taxpayers completing their value added tax declarations and other major taxes like the corporate tax and the vehicle tax.

CAPTCHA Experiment Results

The results of the trial show that none of the messages used in the experiment yielded a statistically significant impact on tax declaration. The interventions, based on others that have been successful elsewhere, were all found to have no impact on the amount declared in this context. Because *all* of the interventions were ineffective, it is hypothesized that it may be that the mechanism (the CAPTCHA window) is not appropriate. The messages were presented prior to reaching the form itself, which may have kept them too separate from the declaration.

The trial, however, underscored a number of important advantages to conducting this type of behavioral research. Despite its enormous sample size, the cost of the experiment was modest. In particular, its cost was lower than the cost of the letter experiment reported earlier, because it only required website code programming changes, which SAT personnel undertook using existing systems and processes. This stands in stark contrast to the large financial and human resource commitments and time costs involved in most reforms aimed at increasing tax compliance, both in Guatemala and elsewhere. As a result, the potential returns generated by Experiment 1 would offset the cost of Experiment 2 many times over.

Moreover, though the second experiment did not reveal a significant correlation between messages delivered via CAPTCHA prompts and the accuracy of tax filing, the CAPTCHA experiment could still positively influence tax compliance in Guatemala by dissuading policy makers from adopting an ineffective strategy. Finally, the experiment generated a rich dataset that may prove valuable in future research. Although not all behavioral research projects will entail the same costs and benefits, Guatemala's experience with these two experiments strongly suggests that developing an institutional capacity for behavioral analysis would prove highly cost-effective.

Further Opportunities for Behavioral Experiments

Building on recent findings, further research could test a wide range of interventions based on behavioral economics to boost tax declaration and payment rates. For example, e-mail messages, cellular text messages, or a combination of the two could have a greater impact than physical letters. Indeed, text messages may be especially effective in reaching taxpayers who lack reliable mail delivery or regular e-mail access.

Further testing could also help tax authorities to determine which specific messages—delivered through which specific media and to which specific taxpayer groups—have the greatest impact on compliance. Beyond influencing tax compliance, further avenues for RCT-based research include experiments designed to

- Test the connection between tax compliance and the provision of public goods;
- Evaluate strategies for leveraging network effects to promote more timely and accurate tax declarations; and
- Gauge the potential influence of individual attitudes and firm characteristics on payment rates.

In each case, sensitivity to the local context is critical to producing empirically robust results that can form the basis for effective national policies.

Conclusion

Institutionalizing behavioral economics research at the national level could enable countries like Guatemala to develop interventions that are demonstrably effective in the local context at a very low fiscal cost and with minimal demands on administrative and human resources. Although policy makers may be tempted to simply apply the findings of international research without testing their local impact, a failure to account for the numerous factors that can influence behavior in a given national context may render such interventions ineffective or even counterproductive.

The potentially positive impact of behavioral interventions more than justifies the cost of experimentation. Based on the costs and benefits of the experiments described above, the Guatemalan Tax Authority could establish a permanent research team that conducts similar impact evaluations and finance this research team with the receipts generated by these experiments.

There is also reason to believe that continuing to conduct new experiments may itself encourage tax compliance. The letter experiment continued to generate a significant positive impact a year after the initial intervention and may continue to do so in the future. It is also possible, however, that its effectiveness could diminish over time as the letters become routine and the perceived threat of enforcement fades. Changing the content of these messages or the medium through which they are delivered may signal that the authorities are continuing to pay attention, and fostering this perception may promote taxpayer compliance independently of the messages themselves.[8]

Technological advancements are further reducing the already low cost and limited administrative demands of behavioral research. The CAPTCHA experiment highlights the limited risk of an unsuccessful intervention. Because the experiment leveraged the tax payment software used by the government's website, it required no physical letters, surveys, enumerators, databases, or other relatively expensive research tools. As a result, its cost was minor even in the context of Guatemala's modest budgetary resources.

Finally, the process of continuous experimentation based on behavioral economics may itself yield important benefits for the tax authority and the government in general. Designing experiments, piloting new interventions, monitoring the results, and developing policy applications can generate important spillover effects. These experiments produce granular data on firms and individuals, which can inform policies in other areas. Additionally, the adoption of cutting-edge analytical methods can influence research and evaluation efforts across the public administration. Creating the institutional capacity for RCT experimentation thus has the potential to generate large returns at comparatively low costs for low- and middle-income countries.

Annex 2A Treatment Letters and Analysis Tables from Letter Experiment to Increase Guatemalan Tax Compliance

Figure 2A.1 Original SAT Letter Used in Guatemalan Tax Compliance Experiment (T1, $n = 6{,}198$)

ALERTA SAT

Guatemala, 23 de mayo de 2014

Chimaltenango, Chimaltenango

Por este medio me permito informarle que de conformidad con los registros con que cuenta para el efecto la Administración Tributaria, usted omitió la presentación de la declaración siguiente:

PERÍODO	IMPUESTO	FORMULARIO
2013	ISR ANUAL	SAT-1411

Por lo antes indicado, se le requiere revisar sus registros y presentar la declaración omitida, haciendo uso de los medios que la SAT ha puesto a disposición de los contribuyentes.

Lo anterior no limita el ejercicio de la potestad con que cuenta la Administración Tributaria para iniciar el procedimiento de determinación correspondiente.

En caso de duda, cordialmente le invitamos a acudir a la oficina tributaria de su conveniencia, donde será atendido y orientado por un analista especializado.

Base legal: artículo 32 de la Constitución Política de la República; artículo 3 del Decreto 1-98 Ley Orgánica de la SAT; artículos 89, 98, 112 inciso c), 112 numeral 6, del decreto 6-91 del Congreso de la República, Código Tributario.

Atentamente,

SUPERINTENDENCIA DE ADMINISTRACIÓN TRIBUTARIA

Source: Guatemalan Tax Authority.

Figure 2A.2 "Behavioral Design" Letter Used in Guatemalan Tax Compliance Experiment (T2, *n* = 6,199)

ALERTA SAT⊣

Acatenango, Chimaltenango

Guatemala, 26 de mayo de 2014

Por favor presente su declaración del impuesto sobre la renta

Estimado contribuyente:

Hemos revisado nuestros archivos y encontramos que usted no ha presentado su declaración anual del Impuesto sobre la Renta correspondiente al año 2013.

Si usted no declara, puede ser auditado y ser sujeto al procedimiento establecido por ley.

Por favor declare en un plazo de 10 días después de recibida esta alerta, lo cual será verificado.

- Para ello, visite: http://declaraguate.gt (Formulario SAT-1411)

Si usted no puede pagar el monto total ahora, podría ser posible que pague en cuotas, luego de preparar su declaración y acercarse a una oficina de la SAT.

Si tiene alguna consulta, contáctenos a través del teléfono 2329-7111. En ese caso haga referencia a su número de alerta: ALERTA SAT⊣

Estaremos verificando cómo responde a esta carta.

Atentamente,

Lic. César Alfredo Lemus Estrada
Gerente Regional Central
Superintendencia Administración Tributaria

Base Legal: Artículos 98,112 y 146 del Código Tributario;
Artículo 3 de la Ley Orgánica de la Superintendencia de Administración Tributaria.

Source: Guatemalan Tax Authority.

Figure 2A.3 "Behavioral + Social Norm" Letter Used in Guatemalan Tax Compliance Experiment (T3, *n* = 6,198)

ALERTA SAT

Chimaltenango, Chimaltenango

Guatemala, 26 de mayo de 2014

Por favor presente su declaración del impuesto sobre la renta

Estimado contribuyente:

Según nuestros registros, 64.5% de los guatemaltecos declararon a tiempo su Impuesto sobre la Renta correspondiente al año 2013. Usted es parte de una minoría de guatemaltecos que no ha presentado su declaración de este impuesto.

Si usted no declara, puede ser auditado y ser sujeto al procedimiento establecido por ley.

Por favor declare en un plazo de 10 días después de recibida esta alerta, lo cual será verificado.

- **Para ello, visite:** http://declaraguate.gt (Formulario SAT-1411)

Si usted no puede pagar el monto total ahora, podría ser posible que pague en cuotas, luego de preparar su declaración y acercarse a una oficina de la SAT.

Si tiene alguna consulta, contáctenos a través del teléfono 2329-7111. En ese caso haga referencia a su número de alerta: ALERTA SAT-I

Estaremos verificando cómo responde a esta carta.

Atentamente,

Lic. César Alfredo López Estrada
Gerente Regional Central
Superintendencia de Administración Tributaria

Base Legal: Artículos 98, 112 y 146 del Código Tributario;
Artículo 3 de la Ley Orgánica de la Superintendencia de Administración Tributaria

Source: Guatemalan Tax Authority.

Figure 2A.4 "Deliberate Choice" Letter Used in Guatemalan Tax Compliance Experiment (T4, *n* = 6,199)

ALERTA SAT-4

Chimaltenango, Chimaltenango

Guatemala, 28 de mayo de 2014

Por favor presente su declaración del impuesto sobre la renta

Estimado contribuyente:

Hemos revisado nuestros archivos y encontramos que usted no ha presentado su declaración anual del Impuesto sobre la Renta correspondiente al año 2013.

Anteriormente, hemos considerado su falta como un descuido. Sin embargo, si usted no declara ahora, vamos a considerar que es su elección, y puede ser auditado y ser sujeto al procedimiento establecido por ley.

Por favor declare en un plazo de 10 días después de recibida esta alerta, lo cual será verificado.

- **Para ello, visite:** http://declaraguate.gt (Formulario SAT-1411)

Si usted no puede pagar el monto total ahora, podría ser posible que pague en cuotas, luego de preparar su declaración y acercarse a una oficina de la SAT.

Si tiene alguna consulta, contáctenos a través del teléfono 2329-7111. En ese caso haga referencia a su número de alerta: ALERTA SAT-4

Estaremos verificando cómo responde a esta carta.

Atentamente,

Lic. César Alfredo Larios Salceda
Gerente Regional Central
Superintendencia de Administración Tributaria
(SAT)
Base Legal: Artículos 98,112 y 146 del Código Tributario;
Artículo 3 de la Ley Orgánica de la Superintendencia de Administración Tributaria.

Source: Guatemalan Tax Authority.

Figure 2A.5 "Behavioral + National Pride" Letter Used in Guatemalan Tax Compliance Experiment (T5, *n* = 6,198)

SUPERINTENDENCIA DE ADMINISTRACIÓN TRIBUTARIA

ALERTA SAT-↵

Chimaltenango, Chimaltenango

Guatemala, 27 de mayo de 2014

Estimado contribuyente:

Usted es un ciudadano guatemalteco y Guatemala lo necesita. Sea un buen ciudadano y presente su declaración anual del Impuesto sobre la Renta del año 2013.

Por favor declare en un plazo no mayor a 10 días después de recibida esta alerta.

- **Para ello, visite:** http://declaraguate.gt (Formulario SAT-1411)

Si usted no puede pagar el monto total, podría ser posible que pague en cuotas, luego de preparar su declaración y acercarse a una oficina de la SAT.

Si tiene alguna consulta, contáctenos a través del teléfono 2329-7111. En ese caso haga referencia a su número de alerta: ALERTA SAT

¿Va a apoyar a su país?

Atentamente,

Lic. César Alfredo Loreal Salvado
Gerente Regional Central
Superintendencia de Administración Tributaria

Base Legal: Artículos 98,112 y 146 del Código Tributario;
Artículo 3 de la Ley Orgánica de la Superintendencia de Administración Tributaria.

Source: Guatemalan Tax Authority.

Behavioral Insights for Development • http://dx.doi.org/10.1596/978-1-4648-1120-3

Table 2A.1 ITT Estimates of Treatment Impacts on Tax Declaration and Payment in Guatemala

Treatment type	Declared (I)	Paid (II)	Log amount (III)
Original SAT reminder letter	0.036***	0.004	−0.098
(SE)	(0.006)	(0.003)	(0.129)
Behavioral design letter[a]	0.043***	0.005	0.348**
(SE)	(0.006)	(0.003)	(0.129)
Deliberate choice letter[b]	0.055***	0.015***	0.268*
(SE)	(0.006)	(0.003)	(0.121)
Social norms letter[c]	0.048***	0.017***	0.241*
(SE)	(0.006)	(0.003)	(0.120)
National pride letter[d]	0.038***	0.011**	0.106
(SE)	(0.006)	(0.003)	(0.124)
Control group	0.117***	0.039***	4.947***
(SE)	(0.003)	(0.002)	(0.077)
Observations (n)	43,389	43,389	2,010

Source: Kettle et al. 2016.
Note: Numbers in parentheses are standard errors (SE). Control group received no letter. ITT = intention-to-treat; SAT = Guatemalan Tax Authority.
a. The "behavioral design" letter included a deterrent "nudge" message focusing on the cost of noncompliance: possible auditing and legal proceedings.
b. The "deliberate choice" letter included a deterrent "nudge" message framing failure to declare and pay as intentional dishonesty.
c. The "social norms" letter included a deterrent "nudge" message emphasizing that most Guatemalans declare their taxes on time.
d. The "national pride" letter included a softer "nudge" message to be "a good citizen," with a "call to action" focusing on the national responsibility of paying taxes.
$*p < 0.05; **p < 0.01; ***p < 0.001.$

Table 2A.2 Local Average Treatment Effects (LATE) of Letters on Tax Declaration of Businesses and Individuals in Guatemala

Treatment type	Full sample (I)	Businesses (II)	Individuals (III)
Original SAT reminder letter	0.051***	0.047**	0.053***
(SE)	(0.008)	(0.018)	(0.009)
Behavioral design letter[a]	0.062***	0.066***	0.061***
(SE)	(0.008)	(0.018)	(0.009)
Deliberate choice letter[b]	0.078***	0.094***	0.073***
(SE)	(0.008)	(0.017)	(0.009)
Social norms letter[c]	0.069***	0.079***	0.066***
(SE)	(0.008)	(0.017)	(0.009)

table continues next page

Table 2A.2 Local Average Treatment Effects (LATE) of Letters on Tax Declaration of Businesses and Individuals in Guatemala *(continued)*

Treatment type	Full sample (I)	Businesses (II)	Individuals (III)
National pride letter[d]	0.054***	0.077***	0.046***
(SE)	(0.008)	(0.017)	(0.009)
Control group	0.117***	0.126***	0.114***
(SE)	(0.003)	(0.006)	(0.004)
Observations (n)	43,389	11,239	32,150

Source: Kettle et al. 2016.

Note: Numbers in parentheses are standard errors (SE). Control group received no letter. SAT = Guatemalan Tax Authority.

a. The "behavioral design" letter included a deterrent "nudge" message focusing on the cost of noncompliance: possible auditing and legal proceedings.

b. The "deliberate choice" letter included a deterrent "nudge" message framing failure to declare and pay as intentional dishonesty.

c. The "social norms" letter included a deterrent "nudge" message emphasizing that most Guatemalans declare their taxes on time.

d. The "national pride" letter included a softer "nudge" message to be "a good citizen," with a "call to action" focusing on the national responsibility of paying taxes.

*p < 0.05; **p < 0.01; ***p < 0.001.

Notes

1. The letter also added a brief mention that taxpayers could pay by installment, in person at a national tax office, once they had declared their taxes online. Most taxpayers are currently unaware of this option.

2. See the SAT website: https://declaraguate.sat.gob.gt/declaraguate-web/.

3. This figure refers solely to declarations under the profit income tax regime.

4. Only 3.5 percent of Guatemalan taxpayers opt to pay the profit tax, yet this tax accounted for about 17.5 percent of the country's total tax receipts in 2015. Moreover, the profit tax regime includes a large number of exemptions and deductions, which could affect the findings of the analysis.

5. The data were fully anonymized, and taxpayers could be distinguished only by broad geographical region and identified as either an individual (a self-employed professional or entrepreneur) or a business (a registered legal entity). Businesses accounted for 25.9 percent of the total sample.

6. CAPTCHA software is designed to distinguish between human users and automated programs, often by presenting a distorted or partially obscured word that a computer program cannot recognize but that a human user can decipher. The experiment used this system to deliver messages to, and prompt responses from, taxpayers using the revenue authority website. Taxpayers in the experimental groups were obliged to complete these CAPTCHA prompts in order to continue the filing process.

7. See the SAT website: https://declaraguate.sat.gob.gt/declaraguate-web/.

8. Numerous studies have shown that individuals and groups change their behavior when they perceive that their actions are being monitored. It is possible that the impact of the "deliberate choice" letter was due at least in part to this phenomenon, which is known in the literature as the "Hawthorne effect." If so, the letter's impact on tax compliance would be expected to diminish over time if the authorities did not continue to signal to taxpayers that their behavior was being observed.

References

Anderson, C. J. 2003. "The Psychology of Doing Nothing: Forms of Decision Avoidance Result from Reason and Emotion." *Psychological Bulletin* 129 (1): 139–67.

Castro, L., and C. Scartascini. 2013. "Tax Compliance and Enforcement in the Pampas: Evidence from a Field Experiment." Inter-American Development Bank (IDB) Working Paper Series, No. IDB-WP-472, IDB, Washington, DC.

Del Carpio, L. 2013. "Are the Neighbors Cheating? Evidence from a Social Norm Experiment on Property Taxes in Peru." Working paper, Princeton University.

Hallsworth, M. 2014. "The Use of Field Experiments to Increase Tax Compliance." *Oxford Review of Economic Policy* 30 (4): 658–79

Kettle, S., M. Hernandez, S. Ruda, O. Hauser, and M. Sanders. 2017. "Failure to CAPTCHA Attention: Null Results from an Honesty Priming Experiment in Guatemala." *Behavioral Sciences* 7 (28): 1–22.

Kettle, S., M. Hernandez, S. Ruda, and M. Sanders. 2016. "Behavioral Interventions in Tax Compliance: Evidence from Guatemala." Policy Research Working Paper 7690, World Bank, Washington, DC.

Kirchler, E. 2007. *The Economic Psychology of Tax Behaviour*. Cambridge, U.K.: Cambridge University Press.

Lamberton, C. P., J. E. De Neve, and M. I. Norton. 2014. "Eliciting Taxpayer Preferences Increases Tax Compliance." Discussion Paper No. dp1270, Centre for Economic Performance (CEP), London School of Economics and Political Science.

Sheffrin, S., and R. Triest. 1992. "Can Brute Deterrence Backfire? Perceptions and Attitudes in Taxpayer Compliance." In *Why People Pay Taxes: Tax Compliance and Enforcement*, edited by Joel Slemrod. Ann Arbor: University of Michigan Press.

Shu, L. L., N. Mazar, F. Gino, D. Ariely, and M. H. Bazerman. 2012. "Signing at the Beginning Makes Ethics Salient and Decreases Dishonest Self-Reports in Comparison to Signing at the End." *Proceedings of the National Academy of Sciences* 109 (38): 15197–15200.

Slemrod, J., and C. Weber. 2012. "Evidence of the Invisible: Toward a Credibility Revolution in the Empirical Analysis of Tax Evasion and the Informal Economy." *International Tax and Public Finance* 19 (1): 25–53.

Torgler, B. 2007. *Tax Compliance and Tax Morale: A Theoretical and Empirical Analysis*. Cheltenham, U.K.: Edward Elgar Publishing.

World Bank. 2014. "Guatemala Economic DNA: Harnessing Growth with a Special Focus on Jobs." First edition, Guatemala Economic Diagnostic for National Action (DNA), Report No. 90491, World Bank, Washington, DC.

CHAPTER 3

Enhancing Child Development through Changes to Parental Behaviors: Using Conditional Cash Transfers in Nicaragua

Karen Macours, Norbert Schady, and Renos Vakis

Introduction

In many low- and middle-income countries (LMICs), young children suffer from profound delays in the development of cognitive and social skills. These delays have serious implications for their success as adults. Indeed, development in early childhood is now understood to be an important predictor of success throughout life (Case and Paxson 2008; Currie and Thomas 2000).

This case study discusses an attempt by Nicaragua's Ministry of the Family (MIFAMILIA), in conjunction with the World Bank, to improve children's cognitive development through a conditional cash transfer (CCT) program. From November 2005 through December 2006, MIFAMILIA's Atención a Crisis program provided households with funding for nutritious food, health care, and other costs related to children's welfare and development. It also incentivized parents to send their children to elementary school and to take them for regular health checkups. Additionally, the program incorporated awareness raising—encouraging caregivers to recognize and value the importance of early-stage education and nutrition.

Building the program around a cash transfer mechanism had two main advantages over traditional approaches: First and foremost, it helped ease the economic pressures that often prevent poor families from educating their children or providing them with nutritious food. Second, it gave parents an incentive to improve the care they provide their children. This behavior change stimulus occurred because the cash transfer depended on associated conditions,

---

This chapter is based on Macours, K., N. Schady, and R. Vakis. 2012. "Cash Transfers, Behavioral Changes, and Cognitive Development in Early Childhood: Evidence from a Randomized Experiment." *American Economic Journal: Applied Economics* 4 (2): 247–73.

such as the children's school attendance record. In this sense, the program was geared toward creating demand-side pressure for children's development. In doing so, it broke with the customary norm that sees policy makers concentrating primarily on supply-side interventions.

Local Context

Historically, Nicaragua has faced multiple challenges that have hindered the provision of basic education and health services, negatively affecting child development. In some respects, the country is still playing catch-up from the decade-long internal conflict that ended in 1990. Nicaragua is the second poorest country in Latin America after Haiti, with more than two-thirds (68 percent) of the rural population living on less than US$2 per day. With the economy highly dependent on fluctuating export prices, many Nicaraguans depend on foreign remittances to increase their household incomes. Children and adolescents are among the most affected by poverty.

Despite this wider national context, important steps have been made in recent years to improve the education and health of the country's children. Child welfare and development is seen as critical to the future development of Nicaragua given that over half (53 percent) of the population is younger than 18 years of age. Under the Nicaraguan Constitution, all children have the right to elementary education. This is reaffirmed in the Child and Adolescent Code. In 2007, Nicaragua took a major step toward realizing this commitment when it abolished fees for school. The government has also taken measures to increase the school system's coverage and design new curricula, as well as investing in infrastructure, equipment, and improved teacher training. Authorities have shown themselves open to experimentation and innovation in early-stage education, too. Around 350 elementary schools, for instance, are affiliated with the Child-Friendly and Healthy School Initiative, a multi-institutional intervention that seeks to provide children with a learning environment that is safe, nurturing, and respectful of children's rights.

The education system continues to contain serious problems and gaps, however. Currently, Nicaragua ranks in the 54th percentile among LMICs in terms of access to education. The national literacy rate is 87 percent among the youth population, which marks a gradual improvement for Nicaragua but remains slightly below other lower-middle-income countries (EPDC 2014). Early-stage education is not exempt from these shortcomings. Among the chief concerns are the limitations of preschool and elementary school access for all children, late elementary enrollment (first grade), and poor teaching quality, all of which are reflected in substandard learning achievement results. According to the latest available data, one in five children (18 percent) of official elementary school age are out of school. Repetition and desertion rates are also high, with Nicaraguan children taking an average of 10 years to complete 6 years of elementary school (UNICEF 2009).

Noneducational factors such as inadequate parenting, poor health, insufficient nutrition, and substandard living environments also contribute to low child development levels in Nicaragua (Verdisco, Näslund-Hadley, and Regalia 2007). At the time of the Atención a Crisis program, for example, more than half (55 percent) of children ages 0–6 years (representing about 22 percent of the population) lived in poverty. Of all children under five years of age, meanwhile, one-third (33 percent) suffered some form of malnutrition, two-thirds (67 percent) had a vitamin A deficiency, and more than one quarter (28 percent) were anemic.

As a result there is a clear need to invest in integrated interventions at an early stage if children are to start off on the right foot and achieve their potential in the long term. Addressing income deficiencies at a household level is one way of doing so. Financial constraints in poor families mean that parents often cannot pay for school resources or cover the cost of nutritious food. Targeted funding can serve to isolate and help resolve these critical impediments.

Policy Options

Theories of skill formation suggest that if children do not have adequate cognitive and social skills at early ages, future investments in schooling and other dimensions of human capital will have low returns (Grantham-McGregor et al. 2007). It is therefore critically important to identify successful interventions as early as possible.

A range of possible interventions are available to policy makers, most of which concentrate on supply-side measures such as provision of preschool education. In many LMICs, however, state-funded education typically begins at elementary school age. Such preschool provision as exists is usually organized on a private, fee-paying basis. Obviously, this restricts access for children from low-income backgrounds. In Nicaragua, nonformal preschool education is available on a limited basis. This is usually run by voluntary educators chosen by the community and is funded from the national treasury or by international children's agencies such as the United Nations Children's Fund (UNICEF 2009).

Food supplementation programs mark another obvious means of promoting early child development. Research into an early-stage nutritional initiative in Guatemala, for instance, shows clear long-term cognitive and employment benefits for those children who received nutritional supplements at a young age (Hoddinott et al. 2008; Maluccio et al. 2009). There is also clear evidence of the positive impact of cash transfers on child development from a study of Mexico's Program for Education, Health, and Nutrition (PROGRESA, later renamed Oportunidades and subsequently again renamed PROSPERA) (Fernald, Gertler, and Neufeld 2008). However, a related research project in Ecuador suggests that household income levels could represent an important factor mitigating poor CCT program outcomes. In the case of Ecuador's Bono de Desarrollo Humano (Human Development Bonus) cash transfer program, the poorest quartile of the children in the sample (ages 3–6 years) registered an improvement of about

0.18 standard deviations in development (Paxson and Schady 2010). Yet no effects were identified among children who were somewhat less poor.

Interventions by the state and other childcare service providers can only go so far. Parental behavior ultimately plays a crucial determining role in the cognitive development of offspring. In this respect, a child's domestic environment exerts considerable influence. Parenting practices such as reading to children, using complex language, and interacting with responsiveness and warmth are all associated with better developmental outcomes (Bradley 2002). In addition to fostering specific learning skills, stimulating activities help children's development by enabling and encouraging them to learn more generally.

To date, policies focused at achieving behavioral change at a household level have tended to be fairly broad-brush. Typically, LMICs such as Nicaragua have focused on general awareness-raising campaigns about the benefits of early-stage stimulation and nutrition. Adult learning programs or school improvement schemes more generally could be considered in this bracket, too, given the positive correlation between parental education levels and child cognitive development.

However, more targeted, behavior-based interventions remain small and experimental. One area where considerable progress has been made over the past decade or more concerns CCTs (Fiszbein and Schady 2009). Significant differences exist between countries and regions in how CCTs are used, yet they all share one defining characteristic: they transfer cash while asking beneficiaries to make prespecified investments in child education and health. The best-known examples are Brazil's Bolsa Família and Mexico's PROSPERA programs, which both cover millions of households. In Chile, meanwhile, CCTs are concentrated more narrowly on extremely poor and socially excluded people. Outside Latin America, CCTs have been employed to reduce gender disparities, as in Bangladesh and Cambodia. They are proven to increase consumption levels among the poor and are demonstrated to be versatile in terms of implementation. For both of these reasons, this policy mechanism is becoming popular worldwide.

Regarding child development, school enrollment has been shown to increase among CCT beneficiaries in country after country. This is especially true among the poorest children, whose enrollment rates at the outset are typically very low. In addition, CCT beneficiaries are more likely to have visited health providers for preventive checkups, to have had their children weighed and measured, and to have completed a schedule of immunizations. Yet the evidence for long-term final outcomes in health and education remains mixed. Despite some promising studies,[1] more research is required to prove conclusively that successes such as higher school enrollment and improved child height lead to future cognitive development and achievements in adulthood.

A particularly important challenge is to better understand what complementary actions are necessary to ensure that CCTs have greater impact on final outcomes. Such actions broadly fall into two categories: (a) policies that improve the quality of health and education services, and (b) policies that help promote healthier, more stimulating environments for children in their homes.

In both cases, behavioral-based measures can serve a valuable supporting function, either by "nudging" parents to use child services more or by encouraging them to change childcare habits in the home.

Considerable space certainly remains for policy experimentation and innovation in this field. One area of lively discussion in the literature is whether poor parents should be paid for children's education or health outcomes, not only for school enrollment or health checkups. Recent experiments with this approach have been undertaken in the United States—for example, the Opportunity NYC and Spark CCT programs in New York City. The latter incorporated students' and parents' collective performance into the incentive structure. The idea here was to see whether group rewards provide an impetus for collaborative learning and tutoring across different achievement levels.

Intervention Design

MIFAMILIA implemented the Atención a Crisis pilot program between November 2005 and December 2006 in six municipalities in rural Nicaragua. The program had two objectives: The first was to provide a short-run safety net by reducing the need for adverse coping mechanisms, such as taking children out of school or reducing food consumption. The second was to promote long-run upward mobility and poverty reduction by enhancing households' asset base and income diversification capacity.

The basic intervention was modeled after an earlier CCT in Nicaragua called Red de Protección Social (Social Protection Network). Under the terms of the Atención a Crisis program, all beneficiaries received payments adding up to US\$145 over the full year. The payments were made bimonthly. Eligible households with or without children received this same base cash transfer. On average, this basic cash transfer covered 15 percent of per capita expenditures of the average recipient household.

The treatment communities were split into three groups, each of which received a different benefit package: (a) a basic CCT; (b) a CCT plus a scholarship allowing one household member to participate in a vocational training course; or (c) a CCT plus a productive investment grant, aimed at encouraging recipients to start a small nonagricultural activity (box 3.1).

The basic CCT combined conditions and financial incentives. Monetary incentives occupy a central place in behavioral economics. Psychologically influential though they can be, the impact of incentives relies heavily on context: their size, the timing and nature of their delivery, and their salience. In the case of the Atención a Crisis program, the first incentive related to school enrollment. Any child ages 7–15 years in a participating household was required to be in full-time education. If the children were shown to be officially enrolled and if they attended school regularly, each household received an additional US\$90 over the course of the year. A further payment of US\$25 was made per child enrolled. MIFAMILIA used data from schoolteachers to ensure that children in participating households met the necessary enrollment and attendance requirements.

Box 3.1 Summary of CCT Treatment Groups in the Atención a Crisis Program

Group 1: Basic. Households in Group 1 were offered a cash transfer, paid to the "titular" (primary child caregiver) every two months. For households with children ages 0–5 years, this transfer was in principle conditional on regular preventive health checkups. Households with children ages 7–15 years who had not finished elementary school received additional educational transfers (US$90 for the year plus US$25 per child), conditional on the school enrollment and regular attendance of those children.

Group 2: Training package. In addition to the basic cash transfer, this second group was offered a scholarship that allowed one of the household members to choose a vocational training course offered at the municipal headquarters—the scholarship plus US$15 per month for lost wages being conditional on the beneficiary's ongoing attendance.

Group 3: Lump-sum payment package. In addition to the basic cash transfer, households in this third group received a lump-sum payment (US$200) to start a small nonagricultural activity. This lump sum was conditional on the household developing a business development plan.

For children ages 0–6 years, the conditionality was linked to regular preventive checkups at a health center.

The program comprised two other treatment groups, both also having strong incentive elements. One of these included scholarship grants for vocational training, which were available to one-third of the participating households. The scholarships allowed one of the adult household members to choose among a number of vocational training courses. Preferably, the recipient would be 15–25 years of age. The scholarship covered the costs of the training, plus the participants received US$15 per month to cover lost wages while in training (for a period of up to six months). The courses were oriented toward skills for income diversification outside of subsistence farming. In addition to classroom education, the program provided labor-market and business-skill training workshops in the participants' own communities. As with the basic cash transfer, receipt of the scholarship was conditional on the beneficiary's ongoing attendance.

The third treatment group received the basic CCT coupled with a grant to initiate or expand an income-generating enterprise. Again, this intervention was also made available to one-third of the trial's eligible households. With a lump-sum payment of US$200, this treatment represented the largest economic outlay of the treatment groups. Beneficiaries received the sum in two stages: an initial payment of US$175 at the end of May 2006, and a further US$25 after survey completion. All of the recipients received technical assistance to select the activity and to develop a business plan. Beneficiaries could choose any viable enterprise activity as long as it was not explicitly agricultural.[2] The nonagricultural requirement derived from a recognized need for farmers to diversify their income-generating activities.

Implementation

The first step of the implementation process was to separate the 106 communities into equal pairs and then into treatment groups. For statistical accuracy, the selection process adhered closely to the principle of randomization. The mechanism for doing so was a standard lottery, to which the mayors of all six municipalities were invited. Through this randomized selection process, 56 communities were assigned as intervention groups and 50 as control groups.

The next step was to determine which households in the selected communities were eligible for participation in the program. Eligibility was decided through means testing.[3] Baseline data on household assets and household composition showed that most (90 percent) of those living in the selected communities qualified for the program. The proportion of eligible households with children under six years old was even higher (95 percent). Local leaders were then consulted to identify possible exclusion or inclusion errors, leading to a reclassification of a small proportion (7.4 percent) of households.

In the end, a total of 3,002 households were chosen to participate in the program. All faced socioeconomic challenges. Four-fifths (81 percent) of the households, for instance, had per capita expenditures below US$1 per day. Meanwhile, only around one-third (34 percent) of the women and just over a quarter (28 percent) of the men had completed elementary school. Children in the sample had substantial health problems, too. Around a quarter (27 percent) of them were stunted, for instance.[4] Their nutritional deficiencies are substantially caused by a lack of balanced diets, with fruits and vegetables accounting for only 5 percent of their food consumption.

The primary child caregiver (the "titular") in each of these households was then invited to enroll in the program. This was done at a community assembly. In Nicaragua, women are the primary caregivers, and most titulares are therefore female. In addition to enrollment, the assembly events gave the program organizers an opportunity to explain how the program worked and to field any queries that participants might have. They also provided a chance to establish a group of promotoras (promoters), who could act as leaders in their respective communities. The role of these local program leaders, all of whom were volunteers, was to aid information flows between the program organizers and program participants. With this in mind the promoters met regularly with the beneficiaries in their communities to talk about the program's objectives and conditionalities.

At the end of each assembly, a lottery took place to randomly apportion all eligible households to one of the three treatments. Each caregiver was asked to randomly draw a ball with one of three colors from a nontransparent bag. Each color matched an intervention package. They learned which intervention their ball corresponded to at the end of the day, after they had already registered to participate. During the assembly, all the household representatives were made aware that only the treatment communities would receive the program benefits.[5]

The process was widely perceived as fair, and participation in the assemblies and lotteries was close to 100 percent. Furthermore, almost all those who took part in the lottery continued their participation in the program.

A key feature of the program's behavioral strategy was that a number of its features gave rise to spaces for social interaction among beneficiaries. The initial enrollment assembly and consequent paydays proved especially useful platforms for connecting and communicating among participants, who could potentially exchange ideas about the importance of varied diets, health, and education. Program participants were also required to take part in a number of local events and talks, ranging from discussions on nutrition practices to workshops on business development, which also enhanced social interactions.

As mentioned earlier, the basic CCT was disbursed bimonthly. The training and lump-sum packages, meanwhile, included a transfer based on a business plan completion or enrollment in a class. The school enrollment and attendance requirement was monitored by MIFAMILIA through data received from the elementary school teachers. For logistical reasons and lack of resources, the regularity with which caregivers took their 0- to 6-year-olds for preventive health checkups was never monitored.

A follow-up survey was collected in July–August 2006, nine months after the households had started receiving payments. The sample included the 3,002 eligible households in the treatment group and a random sample of 1,019 eligible households in the communities that were assigned to the control group. The results were compared against a baseline study that was collected in April–May 2005. A second follow-up survey was carried out between August 2008 and May 2009 (henceforth referred to as 2008). This was about two years after most of the households had stopped receiving the cash transfers.

All three surveys included comprehensive information on household socioeconomic status, including detailed expenditure modules; extensive information on child health and nutrition, including child height and weight; and one measure of child cognitive development, the Peabody Picture Vocabulary Test (PPVT), whose Spanish-language version is known as the TVIP.[6] Social-personal, language, fine motor, and gross motor skills for all children were assessed as well. For children ages 36 months and older, additional tests were carried out. These covered competencies such as short-term memory, associative memory, and leg motor development.

In addition, both follow-up surveys included a report by the caregiver on the frequency that a child displays each of 29 problematic behaviors.[7] Finally, caregivers' observed parenting behavior was registered by the assessor.[8] Many of these tests have been applied in similar populations in Latin America, including in the evaluations of cash transfer programs in Ecuador (Paxson and Schady 2010) and Mexico (Fernald, Gertler, and Neufeld 2008). To avoid reporting bias by caregivers, the assessors sought secondary sources such as vaccination cards to back up self-reported measures such as health checkups.

Behavioral Insights for Development • http://dx.doi.org/10.1596/978-1-4648-1120-3

All the assessors were female. They were selected for their background (many were psychologists, social workers, or in similar professions) and their ability to establish good rapport with small children. During their training, high emphasis was placed on gaining the confidence of the children before starting the test administration and on the standardized application of each of the tests.

Results

A striking observation about the program was the popularity of the CCT approach. Nine out of ten (89 percent) of those eligible for the training package, for example, enrolled a family member in a course. As for the productive investment grant, virtually all of the eligible households took it up.[9]

Participation rates in the two follow-up surveys were extremely high as well, thus ensuring that the results were statistically robust. In 2006 and 2008, 98.7 percent and 97.6 percent, respectively, of the households interviewed at baseline were reinterviewed. Such low attrition rates were achieved through repeat visits to recover temporary absence and through extensive tracking of migrants. In a small number of additional cases, children declined to cooperate with the test administrator, often because of shyness. A dummy treatment indicates that neither attrition nor nonparticipation by children resulted in any selection bias that could significantly affect the final results.

The follow-up survey results showed the CCT program to be effective in improving the health and cognitive development of children in beneficiary households. More than three-quarters (33 out of 42) of the coefficients were positive. Furthermore, almost one-half of these positive outcomes (15 out of 33) revealed improvements of 10 percent or higher. It is worth pointing out that there were no significant negative coefficients whatsoever. Also of interest is the relative similarity of results between boys and girls.

The baseline data revealed that a large proportion of the participating children were cognitively delayed at the outset of the program. The most significant problems concerned language, short-term memory, and associative memory. The Atención a Crisis program showed signs of correcting these shortfalls. As the follow-up surveys demonstrated, the cognitive and socio-emotional performances of the children in the treatment groups were 0.12 standard deviations higher than the control group in 2006, and 0.08 standard deviations higher in 2008. Similar advances were witnessed for health and motor outcomes. In this case, the program effects were 0.05 standard deviations in 2006, and 0.07 standard deviations in 2008. The magnitude of the effects is equivalent to children being cared for by a mother with 1.5 more years of schooling. This compares well to other child development interventions in the region.[10]

On the face of it, there appears to be a clear correlation between the improvements in children's development and parental spending patterns. The treatment households changed the composition of food expenditures, for instance, with caregivers spending a lower fraction on staples and higher fractions on animal proteins, fruits, and vegetables. The level of stimulation that they provided to their children increased substantially as well. Participating households were more likely to tell stories, sing, or read to their children and to have pens, paper, and toys for children in the house. Children assigned to the various treatment groups were also more likely to have been weighed and to have received iron, vitamins, or deworming medicine.

Interestingly, the results do not throw up any major discrepancy between the three different treatment groups, especially in terms of cognitive development. This is surprising because there is a clear differentiation in per capita expenditure between various treatment groups. Households randomly assigned to the basic treatment increased their expenditures (relative to control groups) by 28 log points in 2006, while those that received the basic treatment plus the lump-sum payment registered a rise of 33 log points. The effect on expenditure for those in the lump-sum group continued through to 2008, although less pronounced (8.8 log points). This is predominantly because of the household's investment in productive activities, as was intended. Expenditure among the basic cash transfer group was small (about 2.2 log points). Again, this is to be expected, because the CCT program had finished two years previously.

That the child development outcomes for the higher expenditure group (the lump-sum treatment) were not relatively higher than the outcomes for the basic treatment group could have several explanations. We could be witnessing a result of convexity in the relationship between outcomes and expenditures. However, the survey findings show no evidence of such nonlinearities for most outcomes. It seems much more probable that something other than (or in addition to) the cash transfer explains the CCT program's treatment effects on child development.

So what could these be? One set of possible explanations relate to the unexpected consequences of the program's design and implementation. The idea of the lump-sum payment, for example, was to start a business enterprise. Yet setting up a new venture has implications for caregivers' time. This, in turn, could affect their behavior in relation to their children's development. Results from the study give some credence to this hypothesis. Mothers in the lump-sum recipient group, for example, were shown to have worked 33 more days in 2006 than those who received the basic payment. However, there was no significant difference in the hours the mothers worked in 2008, nor was there any evidence that the lump-sum mothers spent fewer hours taking care of their children than those who received the basic treatment. By the same token, mothers assigned to the lump-sum payment were as likely as mothers receiving the basic payment to read or tell stories to their children.

Another, more likely, possibility is that the program initiated a change in participants' attitudes and habits. The initial impulse for this change may well have been the cash transfer, but the effects went above and beyond the program's contemporaneous income effects. This line of argument is strongly substantiated by the absence of any fade-out of treatment effects among the program's beneficiaries. Two years after the cash transfer had been discontinued, program effects were similar to those seen during the program itself. So, for instance, households assigned to the basic treatment were still devoting a higher fraction of food expenditures to animal proteins in 2008 than they had been in 2006. They also continued to provide more early stimulation to their children and made more use of preventive health care. These results stand in contrast with the results of many other child development–focused CCTs, where the effects waned after the program's completion.[11]

The intense social interactions among beneficiaries observed during the program seem to be a key reason for this long-term behavioral shift. Beneficiaries were repeatedly informed by local leaders who also participated in the program that its goals aimed to drive improvements in their children's physical and cognitive development. This interaction raised awareness and understanding among caregivers about the importance of measures such as eating nutritious food and attending school. Research into behavioral economics suggests that interactions with other program beneficiaries and peer pressure would likely provide additional motivation for a shift in habits (Macours and Vakis 2009).

Another important factor that helped sustain the effects was that the transfers were made mostly to women. It is widely recognized that women are more likely than men to spend household income on food, education, clothing, and other items that benefit children. This helps explain the high compliance rate among program participants. The longevity of effects, on the other hand, would seem to indicate that women are highly receptive to education and information related to child-rearing. This fits with their traditional role of primary caregivers. How women respond to such inputs relative to men remains largely untested, however.

Conclusion

This paper uses a randomized evaluation to assess the impact of a cash transfer program on a large set of measures of child development in Nicaragua, a low-income country. The identification is straightforward. It is based on random assignment, with almost perfect compliance and remarkably low levels of attrition over three survey waves. We show that the CCT program improved child development.

Remarkably, there was virtually no fade-out of impacts two years after the program was ended and transfers discontinued. Caregivers (most of whom were female) continued with beneficial behaviors such as spending more on nutrient-rich foods and providing increased early stimulation to their children. Their use of these inputs went beyond simply moving children along the curves that relate inputs to overall expenditures. This implies that a behavioral shift occurred.

Ostensibly, there is no great surprise here. The design of the CCT was to provoke a change in behavior by placing conditions on the receipt of the cash transfer. Yet two unexpected findings in the program evaluation indicate that something else is going on: The first of these relates to the link between per capita expenditure and child development outcomes. Although one of the three treatment variations received a higher sum of money and invested more in inputs, this did not correlate to substantially higher development achievements. The second surprising finding concerns the changes in the caregivers' behavior, which persisted beyond the termination of the program—albeit at a lower level of intensity than during the implementation phase.

As a result, it is possible to conclude that something other than, or in addition to, the cash was important in provoking behavioral change. One likely cause was the level of social interaction observed among beneficiaries. Another was the fact that the transfers were made to women, who are highly responsive to child-rearing knowledge and practices that benefit their children. Examining how program recipients respond to child-rearing messages and determining which messages have the most significant behavioral impact represent two important avenues of further research. Another research recommendation would be to adopt a more explicit gender lens in the design and evaluation of future CCTs related to child development.

Notes

1. Data from Brazil suggest that a 1 percent increase in height is associated with a 2.4 percent increase in lifetime earnings (Thomas and Strauss 1997).

2. Because of implementation delays, the vocational training courses had not started at the time the 2006 follow-up survey data were collected. They took place in fall 2006. At the time of the 2006 survey, the difference between the vocational training beneficiaries and those of the basic CCT package was hence limited, although the two beneficiary groups might have had different expectations about future skills, related future income, and/or compensation for the time spent in training.

3. The eligibility criteria were determined using the proxy means methodology developed for the Social Protection Network (Red de Protección Social [RPS]) and based on the national household data from the 2001 Census (Encuesta Nacional de Hogares sobre Medición de Niveles de Vida [EMNV]).

4. On average, the height of the children in the sample for their age was more than two standard deviations below that of a reference population.

5. Those who were part of the control group were advised that they could be eligible for a cash transfer in the program's second year if the year-long initiative were extended. In any event, there was a change of national government at the end of the program's first year, and the trial was not continued.

6. The TVIP is the Spanish-speaking version of the Peabody Picture Vocabulary Test (PPVT), a test of receptive vocabulary that can be applied to children 36 months and older.

7. This is known as the Behavior Problem Index. Responses are coded as "never," "sometimes," and "often." In this study, the number of behavioral problems for which a caregiver answers "often" were counted. For a more detailed discussion, see Baker and Mott (1989).

8. Assessors used a shortened version of the HOME score, an index of 11 positive and negative behaviors observed during interviewing and testing (Bradley 1993; Paxson and Schady 2007, 2010).

9. In the 10 percent of cases where MIFAMILIA rejected a family's business development plan, a revised plan was usually successfully submitted. MIFAMILIA provided technical assistance to help with this resubmission process.

10. Paxson and Schady (2010), for instance, estimate that an unconditional transfer program in Ecuador improved child development by 0.18 standard deviations among the poorest quartile of children in the sample, with no effects among less-poor children. Berlinski, Galiani, and Gertler (2009), meanwhile, report an effect size of 0.23 standard deviations for the impact of one year of preschool for children ages 3–5 years on learning outcomes in Argentina.

11. For the effects of other child development–focused CCTs, see Currie and Thomas (2000) and Garces, Thomas, and Currie (2002) on Head Start in the United States; Heckman et al. (2010) on the Perry Preschool Program in the United States; and Neufeld et al. (2005) and Fiszbein and Schady (2009) on the PROGRESA program on child height in Mexico.

References

Baker, P., and F. Mott. 1989. "NLSY Child Handbook, 1989: A Guide and Resource Document for the National Longitudinal Study of Youth 1986 Child Data." Handbook, Center for Human Resource Research, Ohio State University, Columbus.

Berlinski, S., S. Galiani, and P. Gertler. 2009. "The Effect of Pre-Primary Education on Primary School Performance." *Journal of Public Economics* 93 (1): 219–34.

Bradley, R. 1993. "Children's Home Environments, Health, Behavior, and Intervention Efforts: A Review Using the HOME Inventory as a Marker Measure." *Genetic, Social, and General Psychology Monographs* 119 (4): 437–90.

———. 2002. "Environment and Parenting." In *Handbook of Parenting*, 2nd ed., edited by Marc H. Bornstein, 281–314. Hillsdale, NJ: Lawrence Erlbaum Associates.

Case, A., and C. Paxson. 2008. "Stature and Status: Height, Ability, and Labor Market Outcomes." *Journal of Political Economy* 116 (3): 499–532.

Currie, J., and D. Thomas. 2000. "School Quality and the Longer-Term Effects of Head Start." *Journal of Human Resources* 35 (4): 755–74.

EPDC (Education Policy and Data Center). 2014. "Nicaragua National Education Profile, 2014 Update." Data summary, EPDC, Washington, DC.

Fernald, L., P. J. Gertler, and L. M. Neufeld. 2008. "Role of Cash in Conditional Cash Transfer Programmes for Child Health, Growth, and Development: An Analysis of Mexico's *Oportunidades*." *The Lancet* 371 (9615): 828–37.

Fiszbein, A., and N. Schady. 2009. *Conditional Cash Transfers: Reducing Present and Future Poverty*. Washington, DC: World Bank.

Garces, E., D. Thomas, and J. Currie. 2002. "Longer-Term Effects of Head Start." *American Economic Review* 92 (4): 999–1012.

Grantham-McGregor, S. M., Y. B. Cheung, S. Cueto, P. Glewwe, L. Richter, and B. Strupp. 2007. "Developmental Potential in the First 5 Years for Children in Developing Countries." *The Lancet* 369 (9555): 60–70.

Heckman, J. J., S. H. Moon, R. Pinto, P. A. Savelyev, and A. Yavitz. 2010. "The Rate of Return to the High/Scope Perry Preschool Program." *Journal of Public Economics* 94 (1–2): 114–28.

Hoddinott, J., J. A. Maluccio, J. R. Behrman, R. Flores, and R. Martorell. 2008. "Effect of a Nutrition Intervention during Early Childhood on Economic Productivity in Guatemalan Adults." *The Lancet* 371 (9610): 411–16.

Macours, K., and R. Vakis. 2009. "Changing Households' Investments and Aspirations through Social Interactions: Evidence from a Randomized Transfer Program in a Low-Income Country." Policy Research Working Paper 5137, World Bank, Washington, DC.

Maluccio, J. A., J. Hoddinott, J. R. Behrman, R. Martorell, A. R. Quisumbing, and A. D. Stein. 2009. "The Impact of Improving Nutrition during Early Childhood on Education among Guatemalan Adults." *Economic Journal* 119 (537): 734–63.

Neufeld, L. M., D. Sotres-Álvarez, P. Gertler, L. Tolentino Mayo, J. Jiménez Ruiz, L. Fernald, S. Villalpando, T. Shamah, and J. A. R. Dommarco. 2005. "Impacto de Oportunidades en el Crecimiento y Estado Nutricional de Niños en Zonas Rurales." External impact evaluation of the Oportunidades program, National Institute of Public Health, Cuernavaca, Mexico.

Paxson, Christina, and Norbert Schady. 2007. "Cognitive Development among Young Children in Ecuador: The Roles of Wealth, Health, and Parenting." *Journal of Human Resources* 42 (1): 49–84.

———. 2010. "Does Money Matter? The Effects of Cash Transfers on Child Health and Development in Rural Ecuador." *Economic Development and Cultural Change* 59 (1): 187–230.

Thomas, Duncan, and John Strauss. 1997. "Health and Wages: Evidence on Men and Women in Urban Brazil." *Journal of Econometrics* 77 (1): 159–85.

UNICEF (United Nations Children's Fund). 2009. "Child Friendly Schools, Case Study: Nicaragua." Study, Education Section Programme Division, UNICEF, New York.

Verdisco, A., E. Näslund-Hadley, and F. Regalia. 2007. "Integrated Childhood Development Services in Nicaragua." *Child Health and Education* 1 (2): 104–11.

CHAPTER 4

When Winners Feel Like Losers: Evidence from an Energy Subsidy Reform

Oscar Calvo-González, Barbara Cunha, and Riccardo Trezzi

Introduction

Policy makers often face a paradox: they introduce a reform measure that promises to benefit the majority of citizens, yet public opinion swings against the change. Why is it that the beneficiaries of policy reforms act in apparent contradiction to their own interests? Is it simple status quo bias, or are there other factors to consider?

This analysis explores these questions in the context of a gas subsidy reform in El Salvador. Instituted in 2011, the reform was expected to improve the welfare of around three-quarters of the population. It proved initially unpopular, but public support grew slowly but surely after its implementation.

Our empirical investigation sets out to answer two specific research questions: First, what were the factors driving the unpopularity of the reform before and in the aftermath of its implementation? Second, what variables account for the relatively high popularity of the reform two years after it was implemented?

The theoretical literature offers a number of potential explanations. The most obvious is status quo bias, whereby people who are unsure about the outcome of a certain measure prefer to stick with the current system rather than risk change (Fernandez and Rodrik 1991). The political economy literature offers a number of possibilities as well. The relationship between learning about a reform's outcomes and support for that particular reform occupies a number of recent studies, for example (van Wijnbergen and Willems 2016). This is picked up by recent studies regarding barriers to successful subsidy reform (Clements et al. 2013), which highlight lack of information and lack of government credibility as salient factors.

This chapter was adapted from Calvo-González, O., B. Cunha, and R. Trezzi. 2017. "When Winners Feel Like Losers: Evidence from an Energy Subsidy Reform." *World Bank Economic Review* 31 (2): 329–50.

The theme of information provision crops up in country case study materials, too. For instance, widespread media and information campaigns appear to have played an important role in successful reform efforts in countries such as Ghana, Namibia, and the Philippines (Vagliasindi 2013). Case studies from outside the energy sector confirm the importance of providing information to citizens about the benefits and costs of different policy choices (Fritz, Levy, and Ort 2012).

This study aimed to empirically test how information provision and trust in government capacity influence support for an energy subsidy reform. To the best of our knowledge, this represents the first such analysis of its kind.

The 2011 Gas Subsidy Reform

Liquefied petroleum gas (LPG) is one of the most common fuels used for cooking in El Salvador, with around 70 percent of households using LPG in their homes. In 1974, the government introduced a maximum retail price for LPG bottles. As of 2011 the most recent revision to the price of LPG had taken place in April 2008, when the price for a 25-pound bottle (which has an 85 percent market share) was raised to US$5.10. This marked a US$0.95 increase over its previous level, set in 1996. The authorities paid an additional US$8.50 subsidy for each bottle, suggesting a real market price of around US$13.60. The soaring price of LPG in the mid-2000s saw the fiscal cost of the country's long-standing subsidy system increase from around US$10 million in 2004 to US$154 million in 2010 (equivalent to 0.7 percent of gross domestic product).

In an attempt to bring down this fiscal burden, the government introduced a subsidy reform in April 2011. This resulted in the elimination of the price subsidy and the introduction of a compensatory cash transfer. As a consequence, the price of a 25-pound bottle increased to US$13.60, with eligible households entitled to a transfer of US$8.50 per month. To be eligible, households had to consume less than 200 kilowatt-hours per month. Homeowners with more than one property could claim the subsidy only once. Subsidy recipients could either set the US$8.50 against their monthly electricity bill or collect the subsidy in cash through a government-issued card.

The subsidy reform had multiple benefits, with low-income households the most advantaged. Most obviously, around 30 percent of all households do not use LPG as cooking fuel. These are among the poorest in El Salvador and would, as a result of the reform, now benefit from the additional US$8.50 in income per month. Among the poorest decile, two in three (67 percent) of households do not cook with LPG (Navajas and Artana 2008).

The reform was also designed to eliminate regressive and unforeseen impacts of the original subsidy system. Because the subsidy was focused on existing LPG users and because these users tend to be wealthier, the subsidy was disproportionately supporting the rich. Hence, the bottom 40 percent of the income distribution received only 27 percent of the entire subsidy benefit. By setting the new eligibility threshold at 200 kilowatt-hours per month, around 6 percent of households were excluded, the vast majority of which were high-income. Furthermore, the reform's introduction of a market price dramatically reduced the incentive to smuggle subsidized LPG to neighboring countries, which up until then had been a widespread problem.

In summary, the winners of the reform would be El Salvador's lower-income households. The losers, on the other hand, would be wealthier householders who exceeded the electricity limit, owned more than one house, or consumed too much LPG (as the new subsidy covered only one 25-pound bottle per month).

Curiously, however, the public support for the reform did not fall along the lines of this winner/loser dichotomy, as might be reasonably expected. A nationally representative survey conducted in late January 2011 by the newspaper *La Prensa Gráfica* (El Salvador) showed that only 30 percent of Salvadorans approved of the planned LPG subsidy reform (table 4.1). Such was the level of popular dissatisfaction, in fact, that it is judged to have played a role in the March 2012 congressional elections, in which the ruling party (Farabundo Martí National Liberation Front, or FMLN) suffered significant losses.

Some of the criticism was to be expected. Those who stood to lose from the reform, such as LPG distributors, were vocal in their opposition. What is most surprising is that the unpopularity of the reform among the poor—the targeted beneficiaries of the reform—was particularly high. The January 2011 survey found that, of those in the bottom 40 percent of the income distribution, only 28 percent were satisfied with the new policy. Echoing popular sentiment among low-income households, the Archbishop of San Salvador publicly expressed his fear that if the reform was to be implemented "the poor may be left out." In contrast, the same January 2011 study put satisfaction levels among the top decile of the population (those most negatively affected by the reform) at 50 percent.

As the reform became embedded, attitudes began to shift. Sixteen months after implementation began, two-thirds (66 percent) of all survey respondents said they were satisfied with the reform. This was up from 30 percent in January 2011, a couple of months before its implementation. This pattern was observed also among the poor, who went from a 28 percent satisfaction rate in January 2011 to a 68 percent rate in August 2012.

Table 4.1 Satisfaction Rate with Planned LPG Subsidy Reform in El Salvador, January 2011
percentage

Population category	Approval rate
Total population	30
(a1) Bottom 40 percent of income distribution	28
(a2) Rest of income distribution	33
"Losers" or "Winners"	
(b1) Consume more than 200 kWh per month (losers)	27
(b2) Consume less than 200 kWh per month (winners)	30

Source: Calculations based on *La Prensa Gráfica* (El Salvador) survey, January 2011.
Note: The reform would eliminate the liquefied petroleum gas (LPG) price subsidy and introduce a compensatory cash transfer of US$8.50 per month to eligible households (those consuming less than 200 kWh per month).

A few procedural points are worth noting. The reform suffered a prolonged delay between its initial announcement (in June 2009) and the publication of its contents (late December 2010). It also underwent a few modifications both before implementation (for instance, an increase in the eligibility criteria from 99 kilowatt-hours of household electricity consumption to 200 kilowatt-hours) and immediately afterward (such as the inclusion of subsistence businesses as eligible). Reports of bureaucratic and administrative problems also accompanied the reform's introduction. It is possible that these implementation adjustments could potentially have affected individuals' views about the reform.

It should also be pointed out that our incidence analysis is based on householders' legal entitlement to the subsidy rather than their actual receipt of the subsidy. An estimated 70,000 of those eligible for the subsidy did not collect it. Anecdotal evidence suggests that these were relatively high-income households. There is nothing to indicate that that a large number of poor households were unduly excluded.

Data and Analysis

To examine public attitudes toward the gas subsidy reform, we drew on six consecutive household surveys. These were undertaken by *La Prensa Gráfica*, the largest newspaper in El Salvador. One of these was conducted before the policy's implementation (January 2011), while the remaining five occurred afterward (May 2011, August 2011, May 2012, August 2012, and September 2013).

All of the surveys depended on face-to-face interviews. The first five surveys included a total of 1,200 adult respondents drawn from a stratified random sample using the population census as frame. The final survey in September 2013 polled 610 respondents. The samples were designed to be nationally representative with a margin of error of ±2.9 percent and a 95 percent confidence level.

The January 2011 survey was the most comprehensive and interrogated four main themes: individuals' satisfaction with the reform, their level of information about it, their trust in the government fulfilling its commitment, and their political views. In addition, the survey collected information on cooking fuel and electricity consumption patterns, allowing us to identify potential "losers" from the reform. Finally, the survey collected a variety of individual and household characteristics that are used as controls (as shown later in table 4.6).

The surveys between May 2011 and August 2012 followed a similar structure, although interviewees were asked fewer supplementary questions. In the September 2013 survey, additional questions were added to the original subset, with a particular focus on ex post levels of information and the mechanism through which the benefit was received. These two sets of variables are used as part of our later robustness checks.

A descriptive analysis of this dataset provides a variety of general insights into public opinion regarding the subsidy reform. The most important of these is the absence of any link between being a "winner" or "loser" of the reform or between being satisfied or unsatisfied with the reform. In addition, the overall lack of popularity of the reform does not appear to differ significantly across a range of characteristics such as income or the source of fuel for cooking. Some initial differentiations between gender and education levels can be detected, but these are either negligible or gradually lose significance following the subsidy's implementation.

The data appear to support our hypothesis about the importance of information levels. Most of the respondents had limited information and acknowledged this to be the case. In the January 2011 survey, fewer than one in five respondents (18 percent) considered themselves to be well (or very well) informed about the policy change. This revealed itself when only around one-seventh (15 percent) of the respondents could correctly identify the true price of LPG in the absence of a subsidy.

In addition, the well informed were more than twice as likely as the poorly informed to express satisfaction with the reform (54 percent versus 24 percent, respectively). Notably, the well informed did not have the same expectations about the consequences of the reform. Nearly half (46 percent) mentioned that the reform would have at least one positive effect, while a similar proportion (45 percent) cited negative effects (table 4.2).

In contrast, the balance among the ill-informed swung much more toward the negative, with 69 percent seeing potential downsides from the reform and only 13 percent mentioning any upsides. This result may partly be explained by what the psychology literature refers to as negativity bias or positive-negative

Table 4.2 Expected Consequences from the Planned LPG Subsidy Reform in El Salvador, by Information Level, January 2011

percentage

Survey group, by information level	Positive consequences	Negative consequences
Informed people (54 percent satisfied with reform)		
Identify at least one	46	45
Identify none	10	9
Don't know or no response	45	46
Total	**100**	**100**
Uninformed people (24 percent satisfied with reform)		
Identify at least one	13	69
Identify none	40	1
Don't know or no response	47	29
Total	**100**	**100**

Source: Calculations based on *La Prensa Gráfica* (El Salvador) survey, January 2011.

Note: Percentages do not necessarily add up to 100 in each column due to rounding. The reform proposed to eliminate the liquefied petroleum gas (LPG) price subsidy and introduce a compensatory cash transfer of US$8.50 per month to eligible households (those consuming less than 200 kWh per month). In the survey, "informed" and "uninformed" people were self-identified as such.

asymmetry—referring to our natural tendency to process bad information more thoroughly than good information (Baumeister et al. 2001). It is worth stressing that the survey results suggest that information about the reform is linked with a lower negativity bias.

Political priors, our second area of interest, also conform to our initial assumptions. Those respondents who trusted in the government's intention and had confidence in its ability to deliver on the proposed reform proved much more likely to be satisfied with the reform than those who had no such trust (42 percent versus 22 percent, respectively). Satisfaction with the reform was also higher among those leaning politically with the government (44 percent) than among those who favored the political opposition (19 percent). This result may partly reflect people's tendency to assimilate information in a way that supports their antecedent beliefs (Glaeser and Sunstein 2013). In our context, it may simply be the case that government supporters pay more attention to official policy or are more likely to believe in its positive outcomes.

The Empirical Model

Our empirical analysis aims to quantify the effect of different factors on satisfaction with the reform before and after its implementation. The analysis before implementation explores the role of three main factors of interest:

- *Respondents' level of information about the reform (variable = "Information"):* This is a dummy variable taking the value of "1" if the respondent declares to be either "informed" or "well informed" about the upcoming reform.
- *Respondents' level of trust in the government's ability to deliver the subsidy (variable = "Delivery"):* This captures the expectations of getting the subsidy conditional on qualifying for it.
- *Respondents' political partisanship (variable = "Partisanship"):* This is a dummy variable taking the value of "1" if the respondent is a voter of the ruling FMLN party.

Our dependent variable is a dummy taking the value of "1" if the respondent expressed a view that the proposed reform was either a "very good" or "good" idea, and "0" otherwise.

In the analysis after implementation, we have a slightly different set of explanatory variables, as we expect the level of information about the reform to increase after its implementation. For this reason, we consider "informed" to relate to those respondents who correctly report the electricity consumption threshold for the subsidy. The variable "Delivery" now captures whether the respondent effectively gets the subsidy. The variable "Partisanship" remains unchanged.

Following the nature of our dependent variable, we employ a probit model estimated using standard maximum likelihood techniques.[1]

Table 4.3 Baseline Regressions for January 2011 Survey on Planned LPG Subsidy Reform in El Salvador

Variable	(I)	(II)	(III)	(IV)
Information[a]	0.564***	0.526***	0.589***	0.555***
(SE)	(0.103)	(0.108)	(0.112)	(0.118)
Delivery[b]	0.551***	0.588***	0.606***	0.617***
(SE)	(0.089)	(0.094)	(0.097)	(0.103)
Partisanship[c]	0.505***	0.503***	0.561***	0.568***
(SE)	(0.088)	(0.092)	(0.099)	(0.104)
Constant	Yes	Yes	Yes	Yes
Personal	Yes	Yes	No	No
Dummies	Yes	Yes	No	No
Observations (n)	1,032	1,032	1,032	1,032
Percent correctly predicted (PCP)	0.70	0.72	0.74	0.77
Receiver operating characteristic (ROC)	0.71	0.75	0.77	0.80
Akaike Information Criterion (AIC)	1,143.8	1,142.5	1,221.7	1,222.4
Bayesian Information Criterion (BIC)	1,163.6	1,310.3	1,641.0	1,789.4

Source: Estimates based on *La Prensa Gráfica* (El Salvador) survey, January 2011.
Note: The reform would eliminate the liquefied petroleum gas (LPG) price subsidy and introduce a compensatory cash transfer of US$8.50 per month to eligible households (those consuming less than 200 kWh per month). Numbers in parentheses are standard errors (SE).
a. Variable "Information" concerns respondents' level of information about the reform.
b. Variable "Delivery" concerns respondents' level of trust in the government to deliver the subsidy.
c. Variable "Partisanship" concerns whether the respondent is a voter of the ruling party (FMLN, the Farabundo Martí National Liberation Front).
*p < 0.05; **p < 0.01; ***p < 0.001.

Results

The results of our baseline probit regressions are reported in table 4.3 for the January 2011 survey, with columns (I) through (IV) reflecting different regression specifications. The three regressors of interest enter significantly at the 0.1 percent level in all regressions. The estimates of the coefficients on these variables in the different specifications are similar. Results using logit regressions are also virtually identical to the ones presented here. Although the sign and significance of the coefficients in the regressions are informative, the magnitude has no specific meaning. For this reason, we report the marginal effects of each variable, keeping all other variables at their mean values.

The results of the regressions run on the four intermediate surveys show that being informed about the reform increases the probability of being satisfied by around 20 percentage points (table 4.4). We think this is a large effect, especially given that it stems solely from the individual's level of information. Similar effects are found for the "delivery" and "partnership" variables.

It is also possible to estimate the joint effect of the three variables. Although the unconditional satisfaction rate is 30 percent, it increases to 50 percent among "informed people." If we further condition on being confident about receiving the transfer, the satisfaction rate increases to 60 percent. Finally, if we also condition on being an FMLN voter, the satisfaction rate jumps to 75 percent. Overall, our results show that over time the personal characteristics lose power in explaining the satisfaction about the reform in favor of our main regressors.

Table 4.4 Baseline Regressions for Four Intermediate Surveys on LPG Subsidy Reform in El Salvador, 2011–12

| | Survey date | | | | | | | |
| | May 2011 | | August 2011 | | May 2012 | | August 2012 | |
Variable	(I)	(II)	(III)	(IV)	(V)	(VI)	(VII)	(VIII)
Delivery[a]	0.502*	0.233**	1.127*	0.856*	0.599*	0.605*	0.899*	0.965*
(SE)	(0.093)	(0.116)	(0.084)	(0.109)	(0.098)	(0.116)	(0.087)	(0.104)
Partisanship[b]	0.489*	0.463*	0.152	0.135	0.251***	0.269**	0.429*	0.464*
(SE)	(0.087)	(0.104)	(0.093)	(0.107)	(0.090)	(0.109)	(0.091)	(0.107)
Constant	Yes	Yes	Yes	Yes	Yes	Yes	Yes	Yes
Controls	Yes	Yes	Yes	Yes	No	No	No	No
Observations (n)	1,040	1,040	1,166	1,166	954	954	1,104	1,104
PCP	0.62	0.73	0.69	0.79	0.70	0.74	0.71	0.72
ROC	0.63	0.80	0.67	0.85	0.70	0.74	0.69	0.75
AIC	1,364.0	1,314.4	1,152.0	1,000.0	1,166.4	1,188.7	1,286.0	1,341.4
BIC	1,378.8	1,848.2	1,166.5	1,484.7	1,181.0	1,595.1	1,301.0	1,925.1

Source: Calculations based on *La Prensa Gráfica* (El Salvador) surveys, 2011–12.
Note: The reform would eliminate the liquefied petroleum gas (LPG) price subsidy and introduce a compensatory cash transfer of US$8.50 per month to eligible households (those consuming less than 200 kWh per month). Numbers in parentheses are standard errors (SE). PCP = percentage correctly predicted; ROC = receiver operating characteristic; AIC = Akaike Information Criterion; BIC = Bayesian Information Criterion.
a. Variable "Delivery" concerns respondents' level of trust in the government to deliver the subsidy.
b. Variable "Partisanship" concerns whether the respondent is a voter of the ruling party (FMLN, the Farabundo Martí National Liberation Front).
*p < 0.05; **p < 0.01; ***p < 0.001.

Table 4.5 Baseline Regressions for September 2013 Survey on LPG Subsidy Reform in El Salvador

Variable	(I)	(II)	(III)	(IV)
Information[a]	0.202	0.131	0.166	0.101
(SE)	(0.141)	(0.151)	(0.143)	(0.153)
Delivery[b]	1.104*	1.260**	1.096*	1.276**
(SE)	(0.137)	(0.435)	(0.139)	(0.438)
Partisanship[c]	0.337**	0.335***	0.344**	0.343***
(SE)	(0.129)	(0.138)	(0.130)	(0.138)
Constant	Yes	Yes	Yes	Yes
Personal	Yes	Yes	No	No
Dummies	Yes	Yes	No	No
Observations (n)	527	527	527	527
PCP	0.72	0.73	0.72	0.72
ROC	0.69	0.74	0.70	0.74
AIC	621.7	632.3	622.6	633.4
BIC	638.8	747.1	648.2	756.7

Source: Calculations based on *La Prensa Gráfica* (El Salvador) survey, September 2013.
Note: The reform would eliminate the liquefied petroleum gas (LPG) price subsidy and introduce a compensatory cash transfer of US$8.50 per month to eligible households (those consuming less than 200 kWh per month). Numbers in parentheses are standard errors (SE). PCP = percentage correctly predicted; ROC = receiver operating characteristic; AIC = Akaike Information Criterion; BIC = Bayesian Information Criterion.
a. Variable "Information" concerns respondents' level of information about the reform.
b. Variable "Delivery" concerns respondents' level of trust in the government to deliver the subsidy.
c. Variable "Partisanship" concerns whether the respondent is a voter of the ruling party (FMLN, the Farabundo Martí National Liberation Front).
*p < 0.05; **p < 0.01; ***p < 0.001.

Table 4.6 List and Description of Controls for Survey Regressions

Variable category	Dummies included?	Number of dummies[a]
Personal income	Yes	5
Gender	Yes	1
Age	No	n.a.
Level of education	Yes	4
Being "loser" from reform	Yes	1
Cooking method	Yes	3
Head of the family	Yes	1
Religion	Yes	3
Type of house	Yes	3
Number of people in house	No	n.a.
Marital status	Yes	5
Occupation	Yes	4
Type of job (if working)	Yes	11
Urbanization zone	Yes	2
Geographical region	Yes	2
Geographical department	Yes	13
Party running local government	Yes	2

Source: Elaboration based on *La Prensa Gráfica* (El Salvador) survey, January 2011.
Note: n.a. = not applicable.
a. Number of dummies = number of categories of each variable −1.

The results for the September 2013 survey are reported in table 4.5. As for the January 2011 survey, the regressions are run four times, each time specifying a different set of controls (shown in table 4.6). The only two significant variables are "Partisanship" and "Delivery." In all models the variable "Delivery" is significant at the 1 percent level, showing a large impact on the dependent variable. The variable "Partisanship" enters significantly at the 1 percent level in all models except for model 4, where it is significant at the 5 percent level. On the other hand, the level of information is not statistically significant in any model.

The marginal effects are shown in figure 4.1, in which panels a, c, and e show the effects that our three key variables of interest had on the probability of a survey respondent being satisfied with the reform before its implementation in January 2011. Panels b, d, and f show the effects of the same key three variables on the probability of a survey respondent being satisfied with the reform at the time of the final survey in September 2013. The charts track the following three variables:

- *The "Information" charts* (figure 4.1, panels a and b) show how the probability of a survey respondent's satisfaction with the reform changes from declaring oneself as not well informed (on the left, at 0) to being well informed (on the right, at 1).

- *The "Partisanship" charts* (figure 4.1, panels c and d) show how the probability of a survey respondent's satisfaction with the reform changes between a non-FMLN voter (on the left, at 0) and an FMLN voter (on the right, at 1).
- *The "Delivery" charts* (figure 4.1, panels e and f) show how the probability of a survey respondent's satisfaction with the reform changes between those who do not receive the benefit or, in the case of the January 2011 survey, have no confidence that they will receive the benefit (on the left, at 0) and those who do receive the benefit (on the right, at 1).

We want to highlight three main results from figure 4.1. First, the marginal impacts of our variables were particularly important in 2011, before the reform was implemented. This is evident from the contrast in the slopes of marginal

Figure 4.1 Marginal Effects of Key Variables Before and After Implementation of LPG Subsidy Reform in El Salvador

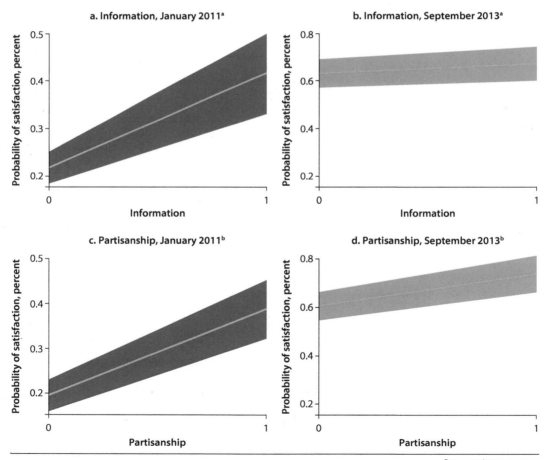

figure continues next page

Figure 4.1 Marginal Effects of Key Variables Before and After Implementation of LPG Subsidy Reform in El Salvador (continued)

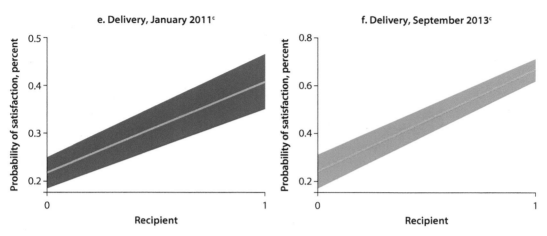

e. Delivery, January 2011[c]

f. Delivery, September 2013[c]

Source: Estimates based on *La Prensa Gráfica* (El Salvador) surveys, January 2011 and September 2013.
Note: Shaded areas indicate the 95 percent confidence intervals around the marginal effects. LPG = liquefied petroleum gas.
a. Variable "Information" concerns respondents' self-declared level of information about the reform, from 0 (not well informed) to 1 (well informed).
b. Variable "Partisanship" concerns whether the respondent is a voter of the ruling party (FMLN, the Farabundo Martí National Liberation Front), from 0 (non-FMLN voter) to 1 (FMLN voter).
c. Variable "Delivery" concerns respondents' level of trust in the government to deliver the subsidy, from 0 (no benefit or no confidence of receiving it) to 1 (receiving the benefit).

effects between the January 2011 charts (panels a, c, and e) and the September 2013 charts (panels b, d, and f). In particular, the slopes for the variables "Information" and "Partisanship" are steeper in 2011 than in 2013, showing that those two variables—whether respondents were well informed about the reform and whether they were FMLN voters—affected the population's support more in 2011 (before reform implementation began) than in 2013.

Second, focusing on the level and not on the slope of the marginal effects highlights how the variables "Information" and "Partisanship" remained highly important throughout, even two years after the implementation of the reform. For example, the marginal impact of political partisanship in 2013 increases the probability of satisfaction from about 62 percent (for non-FMLN voters) and about 74 percent (for FMLN voters). Even more significant is the marginal effect of the variable "Delivery," which in 2013 causes the probability of being satisfied to rise from around 35 percent (of reform nonbeneficiaries) to around 75 percent (of beneficiaries).

Third, it is important to stress that the impact of the variable "Delivery" was much more muted in 2011 (before the implementation of the reform), when a respondent's certainty of receiving the benefit only raised the probability of being satisfied to around 40 percent (note the different ranges in the axes shown). This result underscores the point that factors other than benefiting from the subsidy or not—and therefore of being either "winners" or "losers" of the reform in a traditional political economy sense—are critical to understanding the population's satisfaction with a given reform. Behavioral insights can help enrich our understanding of policy reform successes and failures.

Conclusion

This analysis illustrates how opposition to a policy reform may come not only from the likely "losers" of the reform; those who simply know little about the policy or proposed change may also have a natural inclination to oppose the changes. Traditional political economy analysis of winners and losers of reforms is not enough to predict how these groups will respond to the reforms. This has significant implications for the planning of policy reforms as well as for the need for a communication strategy. Moreover, the salience of various service or benefit delivery mechanisms is an important but often overlooked factor in helping to explain how people think a particular policy will affect them.

In the case of El Salvador's LPG subsidy reform, the econometric results presented here enable us to draw three main conclusions:

- Before reform implementation, the level of information about the reform, the expectations of the government's ability to deliver, and political priors help explain most of the overall satisfaction rate.
- The increase in the satisfaction rate over time is driven by the government's ability to deliver the subsidy.
- Political partisanship had an important effect on the perception of the reform, not only before implementation but also throughout the entire period of analysis.

Overall, our findings suggest that the level of satisfaction with the reform could potentially have been affected by actions to increase individuals' level of information. It is important to stress that such efforts could have played a role without necessarily modifying the content of the reform. In this sense, these findings point to issues that go beyond the political economy of reform as it is often understood (that is, in the sense of identifying winners and losers).

When seeking to understand the success or failure of policy reforms, the findings also indicate that policy makers would do well to explore factors that may affect why individuals consider themselves to be either "winners" or "losers" of particular reforms. Doing so by drawing upon behavioral insights promises to be a worthwhile effort to inform both the design and implementation of policies.

Note

1. Our baseline model can be formally expressed as: $Y_i = \alpha_i + \beta_1\ Information_i + \beta_2\ Delivery_i + \beta_3\ Partisanship_i + \theta^0\ \chi i + \delta^0\ Z_i + \varepsilon_i$, where α_i is a constant term, θ and δ are vectors of coefficients, χi is a matrix containing controls describing personal characteristics of the respondent, Z_i is a matrix of geographical dummies, and ε_i is an error term. The coefficients of interests are β_1, β_2, and β_3. The models are run twice,

the first time specifying a probit regression while the second a logit regression. Following the classical approach of limited dependent variable regressions, we report (for the two main surveys: January 2011 and September 2013) the marginal effects of the three main regressors, keeping all other variables at their mean values. Finally, to overcome the traditional issues of the R^2 in probit/logit models, for each regression we report two alternative measures of goodness of fit: the percentage of correctly predicted (PCP) observations and the "receiver operating characteristic" (ROC) curve that overcomes the arbitrary PCP cutoff to classify the observations.

References

Baumeister, R., E. Bratslavsky, C. Finkenauer, and K. D. Vohs. 2001. "Bad Is Stronger than Good." *Review of General Psychology* 5 (4): 323–70.

Clements, Benedict J., David Coady, Stefania Fabrizio, Sanjeev Gupta, Trevor Serge Coleridge Alleyne, and Carlo A. Sdralevich, eds. 2013. *Energy Subsidy Reform: Lessons and Implications*. Washington, DC: International Monetary Fund.

Fernandez, Raquel, and Dani Rodrik. 1991. "Resistance to Reform: Status Quo Bias in the Presence of Individual-Specific Uncertainty." *American Economic Review* 81 (5): 1146–55.

Fritz, Verena, Brian Levy, and Rachel Ort. 2012. *Problem-Driven Political Economy Analysis: The World Bank's Experience*. Directions in Development Series. Washington, DC: World Bank.

Glaeser, Edward L., and Cass R. Sunstein. 2013. "Why Does Balanced News Produce Unbalanced Views?" NBER Working Paper No. 18975, National Bureau of Economic Research, Cambridge, MA.

Navajas, Fernando, and Daniel Artana. 2008. "Análisis y rediseño de los subsidios en El Salvador" [Analysis and Redesign of Subsidies in El Salvador]. Study, Salvadoran Foundation for Economic and Social Development (FUSADES), El Salvador.

Vagliasindi, Maria. 2013. *Implementing Energy Subsidy Reforms: Evidence from Developing Countries*. Directions in Development Series. Washington, DC: World Bank.

van Wijnbergen, Sweder, and Tim Willems. 2016. "Learning Dynamics and the Support for Economic Reforms: Why Good News Can Be Bad." *World Bank Economic Review* 30 (1): 1–23.

CHAPTER 5

Redistribution in Times of Fiscal Pressure: Using Games to Inform a Subsidy Reform in El Salvador

Germán Caruso, Megan Zella Rounseville, Manuel Sánchez Masferrer, and Kinnon Scott

Introduction

Governments often create subsidies to help the poor and vulnerable cope with price increases of basic services such as energy and water. El Salvador is typical of such a trend. Important though such subsidies can be for the most vulnerable in society, there is a danger that they can become misaligned and distortive over time. This, too, has become the case in El Salvador—spurring reforms to curtail or better target the subsidy schemes.

In 2015, around 80 percent of the population received a public subsidy that helped offset the cost of their electricity and water consumption.[1] The country's subsidy program represents a huge drag on public expenditure and contributes to El Salvador's reputation as one of the region's most indebted nations. Excessive subsidies not only reduce the public funding available for social programs that target the poor (around 37 percent of the population in El Salvador, according to the national poverty line) but also disproportionately benefit those who are economically better-off.

Subsidy reform therefore represents an important opportunity to both reduce the deficit and increase the progressivity of public spending. Such reforms are difficult to enact, however, because subsidies are popular with voters and politically useful for their elected representatives. Rather than rescind subsidies entirely, governments generally attempt to identify more moderate reforms that are politically feasible. The success of such reforms depends in no small part on how citizens and other economic actors perceive the changes. There is, unfortunately, a lack of knowledge about these perceptions and how to measure them.

This chapter is based on Caruso, Germán, Megan Rounseville, Manuel Sanchez Masferrer, and Kinnon Scott. 2015. "Re-Distribution in Times of Fiscal Pressure: Using Games to Inform a Subsidy Reform in El Salvador." Working paper, World Bank, Washington, DC.

To help calculate how such perceptions may play out, policy analysts can use behavioral games. Behavioral games have attracted the attention of social scientists since the seminal "dictator game" described by Güth, Schmittberger, and Schwarze (1982). In this game, a player receives a sum of money and proposes how to divide it between himself and another player. Rather than keep all the money, participants opt to share one-third of it on average. This raises interesting insights about how people's inequality preferences work, as well as how these might be revealed through behavioral games.

In this experiment, we set out to explore the potential of a game-based approach in the context of a subsidy reform process in El Salvador. It adds to previous research mainly by considering two factors that, to our knowledge, have not been previously studied: the impact that the destination of subsidy funds has on people's willingness to forgo a subsidy, and the role that information has in influencing how willing people are to share. We also consider how individual beliefs about government feed into acceptance levels for subsidy reform. Our hypothesis is that people might be more willing to agree to a redistribution of water and energy subsidies if they trust their government and if they know more about where subsidy payments are directed, who benefits, and to what extent.

Local Context

Although El Salvador has experienced comparatively slow economic growth over the past decade (average 2.1 percent annual growth between 2004 and 2014, compared with a regional average of 3.4 percent in Latin America and the Caribbean), it has also made some minor inroads against poverty (decreasing from 34.6 percent to 31.8 percent of households over the same period). One of the main challenges facing the government is a long-standing fiscal deficit, which stood at 3.3 percent in 2015. Public debt, meanwhile, hit 61 percent of gross domestic product (GDP) at the end of 2015—far above the various thresholds for "safe" levels of debt that sit at around 35–40 percent of GDP (IMF 2015).

The government has a public commitment to pursue a fiscal policy goal to improve the efficacy of social programs and subsidies. Reform measures were introduced in recent years to try to square this circle (see annex 5A, table 5A.2 for a timeline). Subsidies of electricity, water, public transportation, and cooking fuel have a long history in El Salvador. In 2015 the reform efforts focused on the first two of these: The electricity subsidy was limited to households consuming less than 100 kilowatt-hours, while those using 100–199 kilowatt-hours lost their previous subsidy. As for water, the subsidy rate now varies according to consumption—from almost 80 percent for households consuming 10 cubic meters to less than 18 percent for those consuming 43 cubic meters. The water subsidy reforms reduced overall subsidy payments, with 3 percent of households served by ANDA (the public water utility) losing the subsidy and 24 percent paying a higher, albeit still subsidized, rate.

Policy Options

Overall, fiscal policy in El Salvador is slightly progressive and has a minimal effect on poverty, recent studies indicate (Beneke, Lustig, and Oliva 2015; Calvo-González and López 2015). Direct cash transfers are well targeted to the poorest households, but they are too small to have much effect on inequality and poverty reduction. Indirect subsidies of water, energy, electricity, and transportation in El Salvador represent a larger share of public expenditure (8.4 percent) than do major social programs (3.3 percent, not counting public services in health and education) (Beneke, Lustig, and Oliva 2015), and they have increased significantly in recent years (annex 5A, tables 5A.1 and 5A.3). Unlike social programs, however, these subsidies are quite regressive: the bottom 40 percent of the population receives only 28 percent of the value of all subsidies, while the top 40 percent receives 54 percent. In contrast, the poorest 40 percent receives 61 percent of the benefits of social spending.

One obvious solution is to target the subsidy payments more toward the poor. Under the current system, only 8.2 percent of indirect subsidies go to those with per capita incomes of US$2.50 or less per day, even though the individuals in this income bracket make up nearly one-fifth (19.2 percent) of the population. However, the political sensibilities of such a reform should not be underestimated. One recent study found that El Salvador has the most politically polarized electorate in the entire Latin American and Caribbean region (Singer 2016). This makes consensus building an uphill task.

For the most part, the motivation for and structure of previous reforms have originated in the fiscal problems or pressure (Inchauste and Victor 2016; Schneider and Heredia 2003; Tomassi 2003). In El Salvador, previous efforts to reduce subsidy coverage have generally resulted in only a small net effect, partly because the reductions focused on high-income households, which represent only a small percentage of subsidy recipients. Nor have these attempts at reform benefited from a clear method for ascertaining people's preferences for redistribution a priori.

Intervention Design

Our intervention was structured around a set of economic behavioral games. The object of these games was to evaluate the willingness with which high-income householders would accept subsidy reforms that affected them directly.

We were particularly interested to know which factors and beliefs lead people to be more willing to accept changes to subsidy payments. One of our central hypotheses revolved around the effect of public awareness. We theorized that those who know more about the subsidy system would be more willing to accept changes. Likewise, we hypothesized that information about the uses of the savings from a subsidy reform would affect people's disposition toward changes in the subsidy system. Finally, we posited that those who trusted the government would be more predisposed to changes in the subsidy system.

We chose four games in total. The first two—the "dictator game" and the "ultimatum game"—are designed to measure general attitudes toward inequality as well as the effect of social norms. In the dictator game, half of the participants received US$10. They were then asked to propose how this sum should be divided between themselves and another player randomly selected among the participants who did not receive money. The amounts to be received were not made public until the end of the session. After participants played the dictator game, they were invited to play the ultimatum game. This is identical to the dictator game except for the role of the randomly selected participant, who can choose whether or not to accept the proposed division of funds. If the recipient declines, then neither player (neither the offerer nor the recipient) receive any funds. All of the results were released at the end of the session.

The second set of games sought to determine how those negatively affected by a proposed subsidy reform (that is, high-income households) might respond to different scenarios. The first game focused on the electricity subsidy. Each participant received US$10 and was then invited to pay an electric bill of US$5. Of this five-dollar charge, three dollars were subsidized. The game involved a significant role-play element: participants actually had to pay the electricity bill in person to a member of the experiment team, who subsequently gave them back US$3, representing the subsidy. This helped tangibly convey the fact that the subsidy represents a real cash payment by the government to the individual consumer.

Participants were then asked to make three independent choices between keeping the subsidy or donating it. Each choice reflected a different end use for the subsidy: (a) on pro-poor programs; (b) on programs benefiting the community in general; or (c) on general government expenditure.[2] After each participant made his or her choice, an option was randomly selected, with the odds of selection proportional to the number of votes each option received. The funds collected were then given to the selected program or organization.

The final game emulated the previous game, only focusing instead on the water subsidy and introducing a variation in information. In this game, participants in half the sessions received statistics on the fiscal situation in El Salvador. They were also informed about the size and significance of the country's water subsidy system[3] and reminded of the regressive distribution of the current system.[4]

Although all the games were played under experimental conditions, we used real money so that the games would be taken seriously by participants and would reflect how they might actually behave in real life. The amount that each recipient stood to gain or lose was therefore sufficiently large to be salient to most of the participants.

Implementation

We defined the target group as adults belonging to the fourth quintile (the second highest income quintile) who work or live in the city and would make up the group most likely to lose subsidies in the event of reform.[5] We limited the study to the greater metropolitan area of San Salvador. This was partly because of the logistical difficulties of organizing game sessions in rural areas and partly because metropolitan San Salvador represents more than two-fifths (43 percent) of the country's adult population.

For the purposes of selection, we divided the population in the fourth and fifth quintiles into three main segments based on their occupational status. The largest segment was made up of formal sector workers, who represent 47 percent of the top two quintiles.[6] Entrepreneurs and informal sector workers constituted another two-fifths (41 percent) of the top quintiles. The remainder (12 percent) did not work because they either elected to be occupationally inactive or were unemployed.

The top income quintiles represent a particularly difficult group to reach through a standard household survey. Many people in these income brackets live in gated communities and worry about high levels of crime. The challenges of developing a traditional sample required us to develop a different sampling strategy. To identify formal workers, for example, we placed teams of interviewers at the General Hospital and at the main administrative building of the Salvadoran Social Security Institute (ISSS), and individuals were approached at the exits of these buildings. The team identified businesses that appeared capable of providing at least a net monthly income of US$600 per household in two populous municipalities: Antiguo Cuscatlán and Santa Tecla.[7] For our sample, we focused on business owners and their relatives, as well as store managers or supervisors where applicable.

Identifying upper-quintile participants who are not involved in the labor force (such as students, retired individuals, and unemployed workers) was complicated because we could not use a residential-based sample—the usual way to capture such individuals. As such, we used four high-end shopping malls as the points of sampling.[8] Our team of interviewers visited the malls during the day (when nonworkers were most likely to be present) and invited individuals to take part in the experiments during office hours.[9]

In all cases, members of the experiment team introduced themselves to prospective participants and explained their affiliation to a university. They then explained that they were running an economic experiment and confirmed when and where this would take place. The invitation mentioned that the organizers would provide money to play in the experiment, some of which would remain in the participant's possession at the end of the session, and that refreshments would be provided. Confirmation of attendance was requested. No specific details of the games were given until participants were seated and ready for the experiment session.

The selection process resulted in a sampling of 482 participants in total. Of these, however, only 330 answered all the questions used in the regressions. To check for bias, we ran a test to compare the results for the 482 participants with the final subset of 330 participants. This revealed that the two groups were not statistically differentiable, eliminating the possibility of a bias due to sample selection.

Once the sample was selected, we split the participants into groups of around 16 people each. Each group participated in a one-hour session. For the most part, these sessions were held in a quiet area of one of the aforementioned shopping malls. At the start, we asked each respondent to fill out a questionnaire. The questions were designed to collect information on individual characteristics that have a proven impact on people's aversion to inequality and their attitudes toward redistribution.[10] Participants were also asked to sign informed-consent forms—a request they all agreed to. In an effort to ensure comparability across sessions, a video recording containing detailed instructions for each stage of the session was played by the session facilitator. Additional directions were given as needed by the facilitator.

Over the course of the hour-long sessions, participants played all four of the economic behavioral games, as described above. Despite not knowing each other previously, participants were interested in discussing the games among themselves. A special effort was made to prevent such interactions because pilot testing of the games shows that conversation among participants affects their responses. At the end of the experiment, participants signed a receipt detailing the amount of money received and their identification numbers. These receipts were put in a separate box to assure participants that the questionnaires remained anonymous.

Results

The headline finding of the experiments relates to the willingness of the well-off subsidy recipients to share or forgo their subsidy payments. The results suggest that most are prepared for a reduction in their electricity and water subsidies if the economic gains of these reductions were used for poverty reduction projects or for the delivery of public goods. Furthermore, information about the regressive nature of the present subsidy was shown to positively affect the present beneficiaries' willingness to either share or forgo their subsidy.

Regarding public awareness specifically, the study revealed that prior knowledge of income distribution and equity was poor. Before the behavioral games started, participants were shown five hypothetical income distributions. They were asked which one most resembled the income distribution in El Salvador and which distribution, if any, they would prefer over the existing one. Only 1 in 20 (5 percent) picked the correct distribution, with most believing that the real income distribution is more evenly distributed than it really is. In general, participants preferred a distribution of income wherein the bulk of the population is concentrated in the middle class, with few people in the very poor or the very rich brackets.

This preference for equity clearly emerged out of the first two games: the dictator game and the ultimatum game. Of the US$10 available, the average offer in the dictator game was US$4.12. In the ultimatum game, the average offer was around US$4.55. Such a difference is expected, because the ultimatum game incorporates social pressure while the dictator game only represents preferences for distribution. These values are slightly higher than average among players of these games in other countries (Oosterbeek, Sloof, and van de Kuilen 2004),[11] suggesting that Salvadorans perhaps prefer a more generous redistribution. The vast majority of participants (93.8 percent) in the ultimatum experiment accepted the offers made in the game. This may well be explained by the relatively high value of the offers themselves.

Regarding the subsidy change in El Salvador specifically, the second set of games confirmed individuals' general willingness to give up electricity and water subsidies. In line with our hypothesis, we found that levels of willingness varied depending on how the savings would be spent. If the savings were to be spent on programs for the poor, for example, more than two-thirds of participants said they would be happy to forgo their subsidies (67 percent for water and 70 percent for electricity). The same responses concerning programs designed to benefit the community were marginally lower (58 percent for water and 65 percent for electricity). In contrast, willingness levels dropped significantly when it was proposed that savings would be returned to the general budget (20 percent for water and 17.5 percent for electricity).

The games revealed that access to information on the importance of subsidies to poor households and on the overall costs of the programs are moderately important. Having this additional information increases the participants' willingness to share their subsidy when the funds were for projects to directly benefit the poor, although the increase is only 5 percent. If the funds are used for public goods, the impact of additional information is closer to 2 percent. On the other hand, access to this information reduced the probability (by 2 percent) that the individual would return his or her subsidy to the government's general budget.

Trust in the government also emerged as important, with higher trust resulting in greater willingness to return subsidies to the government.[12] Moreover, those who believe that the government has the responsibility to reduce inequality were also more likely to share their subsidies. Interestingly, social and psychological characteristics emerged as comparatively insignificant. Personal factors such as risk aversion, altruistic attitudes, being socially mobile, and experiencing an act of criminality have no statistical effect on the level of willingness to share. The only exception is individual self-esteem level, which was found to be negatively correlated with the contribution to pro-poor programs.

Conclusion

The overarching aim of this behavior-based experiment was to test how discussions around subsidy reform in El Salvador could be informed by information on redistributive preferences, particularly among those most likely to lose a subsidy under any such reform. The behavioral games were therefore designed to assess the upper-income sector's willingness to share (that is, forgo an existing subsidy). At a practical level, the games sought to identify how tolerance levels affect individuals' willingness (or lack thereof) to share or forgo subsidy payments in favor of the greater good. This insight is important since, alongside sound economic arguments, people's private, everyday attitudes about equity affect their views regarding subsidy reform.

The findings suggest that certain policy levers could be used to influence reforms that address the equity concerns of current spending. These levers are based on three main factors concerning subsidy redistribution: (a) the destination of the saved funds; (b) people's level of information about the incidence of the subsidies for the poor; and (c) people's beliefs about the role and trustworthiness of the government. In particular, the test revealed that most well-off Salvadorans would be willing to share their electricity and water subsidies if they knew the money would be used to directly reduce poverty or deliver specific public goods for local communities.

The experiment indicates that policy makers would do well to take these three core dimensions into consideration when promoting subsidy reforms that affect the rich but keep benefiting the poor. Sending out a clear message to the population that funds will be used for more socially oriented expenditure, for instance, represents one major lesson learned. Second, subsidy reformers would be advised to consider publicizing more information about the overall cost of subsidies and how subsidies are distributed. Finally, our findings should provide a clear incentive for policy makers to promote greater public transparency and probity to win public trust. As a minimum, the image of the government should be taken into account before designating funds from a subsidy reform for general state expenditure.

Annex 5A Supplementary Tables

Table 5A.1 Shares of Population Receiving Electricity and Water Subsidies in El Salvador, by Income Quintile, 2014
percentage

Income quintile	Second-tier electricity subsidy[a]	First-tier electricity subsidy[b]	Water subsidy
1	88	76	12
2	89	72	28
3	88	64	39
4	82	56	49
5	67	39	66

Source: 2014 National Household Survey (EHPM) data.
Note: Income quintiles range from 1 (poorest) to 5 (richest).
a. Second-tier subsidy applies to households with consumption of 199 kilowatt-hours or less (extended temporarily to 299 kilowatt-hours in 2011).
b. First-tier subsidy applies to households with monthly consumption of 99 kilowatt-hours or less.

Table 5A.2 Timeline of Public Subsidies in El Salvador, by Type, 2004–16

Subsidy type	2004	2005	2006	2007	2008	2009	2010	2011	2012	2013	2014	2015	2016
Water	All HHs					Households with consumption of up to 40 m³							Up to 40 m³ (modified schedule)
Electricity		HHs with monthly consumption of up to 199 kWh						Up to 299 kWh	Up to 199 kWh			Up to 99 kWh	
LPG (propane)	All consumers (regulated price of US$4.10)				All consumers (price US$5.10)			Targeted to HHs with monthly consumption of up to 199 kWh		Targeted (with ID card, electricity card)			Targeted, using only ID card
Public transportation	No subsidy			Monthly US$400 per bus or US$200 per minibus		Monthly US$500 per bus or US$250 per minibus		Monthly US$750 per bus or US$375 per minibus		Monthly US$400 per bus or US$200 per minibus			

Source: World Bank.

Note: HHs = households; kWh = kilowatt-hours; LPG = liquefied petroleum gas; m³ = cubic meters.

Table 5A.3 Expenditure on Subsidies of Public Services in El Salvador, by Type, 2009–15
US$, millions

Subsidy type	2009	2010	2011	2012	2013	2014	2015[a]
LPG	83	136	164	136	139	104	75
Electricity	118	111	115	201	177	169	124
Water	50	60	63	65	71	65	55
Transportation	79	48	57	64	56	39	39
Total	331	355	398	465	442	420	293
Share of GDP (%)	1.6	1.7	1.7	2.0	1.8	1.7	1.1

Sources: Cerritos and Aguilar 2015; IMF 2015.
Note: LPG = liquefied petroleum gas.
a. 2015 expenditures estimated for water, LPG, and transportation subsidies; actual expenditure for electricity subsidies.

Notes

1. This was true at the time of the experiment (in mid-2015) that this chapter describes. At the end of 2015, the government reformed the subsidy scheme, and in 2016 only 61.2 percent of individuals received it.

2. To make the choices clear and concrete, specific programs were chosen for each scenario: Techo El Salvador (http://www.techo.org/paises/elsalvador/) for the first choice; the local firefighters for the second choice; and a contribution to the general fund for the government at the Ministry of Finance for the third choice.

3. For example, participants were told that expenditure on the water subsidy was equivalent to the construction of two large hospitals or the annual costs of running the country's school uniforms and school materials' programs.

4. To highlight the regressive nature of the subsidy, it was emphasized that many poor households do not receive a payment (because they were not connected to the grid), while most upper-income households do (only 3 percent of these users do not receive a subsidy).

5. According to El Salvador's 2014 national household survey (Encuesta de Hogares de Propósitos Múltiples, or EHPM), the daily labor income of an individual of the fourth quintile is US$21.60.

6. We define workers in formal employment as those with an affiliation to the Salvadoran Social Security Institute (ISSS).

7. A net monthly income of US$600 marks the cutoff of the fourth quintile. The businesses chosen were high-volume general stores, drugstores, and well-identified specialized stores with an established clientele.

8. The selected malls were the main shopping areas in the municipalities of San Salvador, Antiguo Cuscatlán, Santa Tecla, and Soyapango.

9. Inevitably, some formal workers were included in this sample. Although this undermines the idea of a probability sample, the impact of this on the analysis was mitigated by keeping the sample proportional to the sizes of the three groups.

10. The questions included information on demographic and socio characteristics, risk aversion, and inequality aversions, as well as opinions on the causes of poverty, the role of government in reducing inequality, the ability of the government in reducing inequality, and confidence in the government in terms of poverty reduction.

In addition, information was collected about psychological characteristics (such as self-efficacy and empowerment), experience with crime and violence, attitudes toward justice and equality, and knowledge of subsidies in El Salvador.

11. Note that the samples in other studies (Oosterbeek, Sloof, and van de Kuilen 2004) are of all income groups, while the Salvadoran sample was made up of only those in the top two income quintiles.

12. Trust is a coefficient that sums four subcategories that range from 1 to 10 indicating trust in the executive power, trust in the judicial system, trust in the congress, and trust in the police.

References

Beneke, Margarita, Nora Lustig, and José Andrés Oliva. 2015. "El Impacto de los Impuestos y el Gasto Social en la Desigualdad y la Pobreza en El Salvador" [The Impact of Taxes and Social Spending on Inequality and Poverty in El Salvador]. Working Paper No. 26, Commitment to Equity (CEQ) Project of the Center for Inter-American Policy and Research (CIPR), the Inter-American Dialogue, the Center for Global Development, and Department of Economics, Tulane University, New Orleans.

Calvo-González, Oscar, and J. Humberto López. 2015. "El Salvador: Building on Strengths for a New Generation." Systematic Country Diagnostic, World Bank, Washington, DC.

Cerritos, Mónica, and Gonzalo Aguilar. 2015. *Efectos de las transferencias y los subsidios sobre la pobreza y la distribución del ingreso en El Salvador* [The Effects of Transfers and Subsidies on Poverty and Income Distribution in El Salvador]. San Salvador: National Foundation for Development (FUNDE).

Güth, Werner, Rolf Schmittberger, and Bernd Schwarze, 1982. "An Experimental Analysis of Ultimatum Bargaining." *Journal of Economic Behavior & Organization* 3 (4): 367–88.

IMF (International Monetary Fund). 2015. World Economic Outlook (database). April, IMF, Washington, DC. https://www.imf.org/external/pubs/ft/weo/2015/02/weodata/index.aspx.

Inchauste, Gabriela, and David G. Victor, eds. 2016. *The Political Economy of Energy Subsidy Reform*. Directions in Development Series. Washington, DC: World Bank.

Oosterbeek, Hessel, Randolph Sloof, and Gijs van de Kuilen. 2004. "Cultural Differences in Ultimatum Game Experiments: Evidence from a Meta-Analysis." *Experimental Economics* 7 (2): 171–88.

Schneider, Ben Ross, and Blanca Heredia, eds. 2003. *Reinventing Leviathan: The Politics of Administrative Reform in Developing Countries*. Miami, FL: University of Miami North-South Center Press.

Singer, Matthew. 2016. "Elite Polarization and the Electoral Impact of Left-Right Placements: Evidence from Latin America, 1995–2009." *Latin American Research Review* 51 (2): 174–94.

Tommasi, Mariano. 2003. "Crises, institutions politiques et réformes politiques: le bon, le mauvais et l'affreux" [Crises, Political Institutions and Political Reforms: The Good, the Bad, and the Awful]. *Revue d'économie du développement* 11 (2): 49–81.

CHAPTER 6

Lessons Learned from Implementing Behaviorally Informed Pilots

Laura Zoratto, Oscar Calvo-González, and Oliver Balch

Introduction

This chapter distills some of the lessons we learned during the preparation and implementation of the randomized control trials (RCTs) described in this volume. It covers the steps the project teams followed in applying the tools from behavioral economics (BE) to a variety of public policy issues—from project preparation to pilot implementation and results analysis.

Our focus is on describing the practical challenges that we have faced when applying behavioral insights in a development context and how we approached those challenges. In doing so, our goal is not to provide any sort of "best practice" advice but simply to illustrate that the application of behavioral insights is possible in contexts where government capacity constraints are more acute than in the higher-income countries where the application of behavioral insights in policy got its start.

Our work focused on Central America because the activities reported here resulted from a decision by the World Bank's Country Management Unit for Central America to explore the potential for applying behavioral insights in its work program. The management decision left open which sectors the activities would focus on or the modalities of engagement. In fact, there was a deliberate effort to diversify the sectors and the partnerships because these were meant to be pilot activities. As pilot activities, they were also intended to be relatively quick to implement. In addition, they ought to be able to show measurable

---

This chapter is based on interviews with members of the World Bank teams who carried out some of the activities described in the previous chapters.

results so that there could be little doubt about their impact or lack thereof. In short, the approach followed was much in keeping with the spirit of testing, learning, and adapting.

Project Preparation

Each of the activities that we undertook involved some preparatory work, often related to the need to introduce the concepts and practice of applying behavioral insights in policy making, to ensure that counterparts are fully committed to the approach, and to select concrete and tractable problems to tackle. The subsections below discuss in more detail these three essential steps when initiating a behavior-led policy intervention.

Step 1: Enhance Awareness about Behavioral Insights in Policy Making

Although awareness of BE theory is growing in certain policy-making circles, it remains a novel concept for many. Even in cases where policy makers are aware of behavior-influenced approaches, their knowledge may be incomplete. At the outset of any behavior-led policy process, therefore, it is essential to provide a basic introduction to key BE concepts, methodologies, and principles governing implementation.

In this vein, the World Bank organized a workshop on behavioral insights (BI) during the Inter-American Conference for Mayors and Local Authorities in Miami in June 2013. ideas42—a nonprofit think tank that works with foundations, private companies, and government agencies to apply BI theory in practice—gave an introductory presentation. The Bank team also provided an overview on the policy implications of behaviorally informed policies. The Costa Rican water-use reduction program (chapter 1) emerged as a direct outcome of this workshop.

In Guatemala, meanwhile, the Bank's country economist undertook the initial BI-related discussions concerning tax compliance (chapter 2). Between May and October 2013, the country economist initiated one-on-one meetings with officials of the Guatemalan central bank, the finance ministry, the tax authority, and other relevant opinion formers to seed understanding and interest in this alternative policy approach. After this six-month period, the country manager had achieved sufficient buy-in to arrange a high-level meeting with both the cabinet of the finance ministry and the executive board of the tax authority. A subject expert from the United Kingdom's Behavioural Insights Team (BIT) was invited to present alongside him on these occasions.

One lesson that clearly emerges from all the case examples is the need to work with counterparts who understand the potential value of BE approaches. Imposing it on skeptics is problematic and unlikely to result in success. That said, policy makers who are initially skeptical about BE-based interventions often warm to the idea through a patient process of fact-based, practice-oriented discussions.

One of the main benefits of a behavior-led approach to policy is the comparative speed with which pilots can be designed and implemented. However, the relative novelty of BE theory, and particularly its application to policy making, means that the initial phase may take considerable time. In the case of the Costa Rica water-use project, six months unfolded between initial contact with the country counterpart (the Municipality of Belén) and the pilot's implementation. In Guatemala, in contrast, the process of raising awareness alone took six months. It then took another six months to design and commence implementation of the pilot tax-compliance program. This initial phase of enhancing awareness of the potential for applying behavioral insights in public policy is essential, however, because it saves time and improves outcomes in the long run.

Step 2: Ensure Counterpart Buy-In

It was useful to provide relevant examples of results-based interventions wherever possible. Simply advocating the general value of BE theory to policy making is usually not enough. Instead, counterparts need to see how behaviorally influenced approaches have worked elsewhere and to become aware of their positive impacts. In this way, the relevance of BE theory to their own situations is established. Furthermore, the natural skepticism they may feel toward BE as a new approach is softened. Counterparts' enthusiasm also increases when they understand the low investment required and high cost-benefit ratio.

Early experience in the United Kingdom suggests that civil servants working with policy implementation are easier to convince than policy makers. This is due to the continual pressure on operational-level staff to innovate to achieve efficiencies and deliver improved results. When the country's BIT first approached senior representatives in the Department of Pensions, for instance, these policy makers were cautious about the use of BE theory. It was not until they observed the positive results from the BIT's intervention in a related project that attitudes changed.

Needless to say, it is easier to find comparable examples in certain policy areas than in others. Taxation, for instance, is a subject that has attracted considerable experimentation by behavioral economists to date. As a consequence, a considerable number of case studies now exist on which to draw.[1] The BIT, for instance, has shown that the use of social norms to encourage the payment of tax debts led to an increase in payments of up to 15 percent within one month. The British government estimates that a national rollout of the policy would provide around £30 million (US$48 million) of extra revenue each year (BIT 2012). For its part, the World Bank team found that the case examples that generated the most interest among counterparts were those that were low-cost and showed quick results in politically uncomplicated or uncontroversial areas such as tax collection rates. Moreover, the monetary gains from interventions in this area also held considerable appeal.

Ideally, test examples derive from pilots in low- and middle-income countries (LMICs). At this nascent stage of BE's trajectory, however, it is realistic to assume that most case study data will originate from projects in high-income countries.

It is possible to extrapolate broad conclusions from these trials, but it should not be assumed that the results will be the same in an LMIC context.

Step 3: Focus on Solving Genuine Policy Problems

Counterparts need to trust that a behavior-led pilot is not experimentation for the sake of experimentation. A comprehensive literature review and other background research may enable World Bank teams and governments to identify policy problems where behavior-oriented approaches could make a meaningful contribution. Local policy makers are invariably best positioned to make specific judgments as to which problems have a behavioral component and, of these, which might benefit most from a BE-based intervention.

Where possible, it is useful to encourage an early dialogue with counterparts to identify relevant problem areas. The mayoral meeting in Miami in June 2013 included exactly this kind of forum for discussion, with time given to the participating mayors to brainstorm issues in their municipalities. The mayor of Belén, Costa Rica, immediately identified the issue of water consumption in wealthy districts as an issue where behavior-influenced policies could make an impact. In Cariari, a wealthy neighborhood in the Belén district, for example, consumption levels average 40 cubic meters per month, with highs of up 54 cubic meters per month (as recorded in February 2013). This compares with a mean of 22 cubic meters per month for the city as a whole. Traditional policy measures such as awareness-raising and price increases had proved unsuccessful. Moreover, policy makers' hands were tied, with local governments prevented by law from increasing prices beyond recovering costs. The critical nature of the problem was highlighted by a recent study pointing to the possibility of water shortages by 2030 if action is not taken.

Meanwhile, the problem of low payment of taxes in Guatemala was only too obvious. Guatemala has the lowest government revenues in the world relative to the size of its economy, and consequently its per capita spending on the social sectors is also among the lowest as a share of gross domestic product (GDP). Unlike other countries with low tax-to-GDP ratios, Guatemala lacks significant nontax revenue sources. Yet any attempts to reform the tax system or introduce legislation to boost tax revenues are stymied by a lack of political consensus in Congress. The problem of low tax revenues, coupled with the obstacles in passing new laws, makes the issue doubly difficult. On the flip side, demand for an alternative approach to traditional policy making was accordingly high.

Required Skills and Associated Challenges during Project Preparation

Conceptual and Interpersonal Capability

It is useful if the Bank's teams can clearly articulate BE concepts and convincingly demonstrate how they relate to policy areas, thus helping to solidify the idea. In several of the case studies in this volume, the idea of a BE-based project began to gain real momentum only after a government minister was persuaded of the concept. Good interpersonal skills are a vital asset, too. In all of the case study examples, project coordinators showed an ability to build a network of internal champions and collaborators, all of whom shared a similar vision and who could collectively generate institutional momentum for a pilot initiative.

Policy Experience

Where possible, previous experience in behavior-influenced policy design and implementation is preferable. Such experience not only provides valuable insights as to what does and does not work but also gives project proponents credibility when initially discussing the application of BE theory with counterparts. For instance, the project coordinator for the Costa Rica pilot was able to identify a World Bank water specialist who had worked on a water-use reduction project involving the use of short message service (SMS)-based communications. She invited the specialist to Costa Rica in November 2013 to present his experience to the mayor of Belén as well as to senior executives in the local water utility.

In some circumstances, it may be appropriate for the Bank's representatives to draw on the expertise of external organizations. The Bank team called on the support of ideas42 and the BIT in the early phase of its pilot programs in Costa Rica and Guatemala, respectively. In the case of Nicaragua, the pilot coordinator worked closely with a childhood development specialist at a local nongovernmental organization (NGO) who had expertise in behavioral thinking in the field of early education.

Opportunities for individuals within the Bank to increase their knowledge of BE theory could be considered, too. In October 2013, the project coordinators for the Costa Rica and Guatemala programs spent three days with the BIT in London. This one-on-one training session enabled the Bank's representatives to ask highly specific and practice-oriented questions about project design, implementation, and evaluation. The Bank team also invited the BIT's head of research to give a presentation at the annual retreat of the group of country economists working on Latin America, which helped raise internal awareness of BE theory, particularly in the context of policy innovation.

Associated Challenges

Gaining Counterpart Support

As stated above, achieving initial buy-in from the counterpart can represent a challenge in some instances. This was not the case in the Costa Rica pilot because the municipality's mayor was driving the program from the start. The mayor also had the active support of the water utility, which could see the value of the intervention most clearly. Because both parties were working together on the project from its inception, a strong sense of local ownership characterized the pilot throughout. The ideal should be that the counterpart feels that it is their project, not the World Bank's.

In contrast, the Bank's team needed to invest considerable time and energy to win over key project participants in Guatemala. This was to be expected given the relatively nascent nature of behavior-oriented policy making.

In this case, the Bank's project coordinator secured the support of a key technical adviser with the Guatemalan Tax Authority, who in turn advocated for the pilot with key decision makers internally. Using solid case study examples and reputable subject experts to present evidence is an effective way of building credibility. In the case of Guatemala, for example, the Bank's ability to draw in an experienced third party like the BIT gave the counterparty additional confidence. Demonstrating tangible outcomes from similar interventions elsewhere also proves a powerful persuader. By the same token, counterparts need to be assured that the Bank is not presenting an off-the-shelf approach and that they will have an active role in the design and implementation of any pilot.

Overcoming Resource Constraints

Despite emerging evidence in the literature, the use of behavioral tools in LMIC contexts remains rare. Indeed, before the World Bank's pilots, few if any examples existed of behavioral interventions by subnational governments in LMICs. In part, this dearth of cases may reflect the perception that governments in LMICs, especially subnational governments, lack the infrastructure and technological tools needed to successfully implement and track behavioral interventions.

The pilot coordinators have all reported problems relating to limitations of local resources and expertise, particularly with respect to BE theory. Supplementing resource gaps with external support, especially at the policy design stage, may be necessary in some cases. However, resource needs are relatively small for BE-related interventions and, while not ideal, resource shortages should not be viewed as an unassailable hindrance other than in the most extreme cases.

Project Design and Implementation

As in the preparation stage, project design and implementation of a behaviorally informed policy intervention also involve several primary steps.

Step 1: Complete Context-Specific Research

Any policy intervention requires a degree of baseline research at the outset. Project proponents need to ensure they have a comprehensive understanding of BE theory and how it applies to the policy problem in question. In addition, knowledge of the local context in the proposed project area is essential. It is useful for project coordinators to gain a strong initial understanding of how socioeconomic, cultural, and other factors influence behavioral norms. The outcome of this initial research project should lead to a well-evidenced hypothesis of the key behavioral issues at play. Ideally, it should also result in an initial list of viable interventions.

Literature Review

Although the application of BE theory to public policy remains relatively new, it already boasts a large and growing corpus of academic research. In addition, the literature demonstrates a gradual shift from theoretical discussions to the analysis of empirical data based on real-life case studies. Some issues, such as tax, health, and social policy, are particularly well represented in the literature and merit attention. In other areas, relevant case study material remains scarce. By way of a benchmark, the BIT typically starts most projects with a four- to five-page literature review that summarizes the evidence on behavioral insights on a specific topic.

Focus Groups

Focus groups enable the project coordinator to flesh out insights gleaned from a preliminary literature review. It also provides an early chance to ground any initial insights in the local context.

The water-use reduction project in Belén, Costa Rica, provides a good example of how such focus groups might work. The project coordinators invited a cross-section of people from the target community to discuss the issue of water consumption. Four focus groups were selected in total, each comprising five to six people. Special emphasis was placed on making the groups as diverse as possible, ensuring that representatives from across the project's target audiences were involved.

The discussion was structured around 20 questions that sought to tease out insights on issues such as people's current habits regarding water use (washing, cleaning, gardening, and so on); attitudes toward water and water consumption in general (for example, perceptions of water availability and views on the environment); and views on the potential effectiveness of the possible "nudges" under consideration. The focus groups enabled the project coordinators to draw up the hypothesis that consumers did not pay attention in the bill to how much water they consumed, and to target their intervention accordingly.

Firsthand Research

In some instances, it may prove essential to carry out firsthand research. This provides valuable insights into how systems work in practice (from the perspectives of both the implementer and the user) and may well yield ideas for areas of intervention that have not previously been considered. BIT staff members, for example, worked for several days per week over several weeks inside a Jobcentre (an employment service provider through the U.K. Department for Work and Pensions) to better understand its daily routine and bottlenecks. Likewise, the team leading one of the BIT's tax revenue projects was physically embedded for a year with the tax authorities.

In each case, the knowledge provided by this hands-on research enabled the project designers to refine subsequent interventions and to modify the systems in place. On the downside, this level of involvement can potentially prolong the research phase considerably and increase costs.

Step 2: Identify Precise Behavior Changes

Behavioral theory takes as its starting point two systems of decision making: "automatic" (fast, reflective, and associative) and "reflexive" (slow, conscious, serial, and analytical).[2] The two systems combine to permit quick, instinctive thought processes, on the one hand, and deep, powerful deliberation on the other hand. However, both systems are liable to biases and failures.

BE theory plays to the typical propensities toward bias in our automatic decision-making processes. Thaler and Sunstein (2008) identify a range of biases (associated with heuristics, or rules of thumb) upon which nudges can prove effective:

- *Anchoring and adjustment:* comparing, then guessing
- *Availability:* perceived popularity or rarity
- *Representativeness:* stereotyping and comparison
- *Optimism and overconfidence:* under- or overestimation or complacency
- *Loss aversion:* holding on to things or resistance
- *Status quo bias:* inertia, default to no action
- *Framing:* orientation, accentuation, presentation, styling
- *Temptation:* greed, ego, short-term reward
- *Mindlessness:* negligence, avoidance, not concentrating
- *Self-control strategies:* habits and routines to counter weaknesses
- *Herd mentality:* conforming, mob instinct, safety in numbers
- *Spotlight effect:* anxiety, pressure, thinking "everyone's watching my decision," fear of making errors
- *Priming:* being made ready or prepared before thinking and deciding, such as through visualization; role modeling; building belief; and offering methods, not just directions
- *Stimulus response compatibility*: overlays other nudges via heuristics such as the design of signage or language, so that it looks and seems appropriate for the message it conveys
- *Feedback:* overlays other nudges by giving the respondent time during and after thinking or decisions to adjust or assess the experience

Different policy problems will relate to one or more of these biases. Having identified which ones are most relevant, the BIT recommends a basic framework to help determine which specific interventions might be most appropriate. The framework emphasizes four practically minded principles, abbreviated as EAST (Easy, Attractive, Social, and Timely) (box 6.1).

The Central American pilots deployed a range of nudge tactics. The Guatemalan example followed other tax-oriented initiatives in mixing positive messaging (such as taxpayers' contribution to nation building) with deterrents (such as the threat of fines).

Social norms proved popular in all the pilots. In the Costa Rica pilot, for example, residents were informed through their water bills about how their individual consumption patterns compared with the averages in their neighborhood or in the municipality as a whole.

Some interventions also include explicit prompts to action. In the water use reduction pilot in Belén, Costa Rica, for example, one of the intervention groups

Box 6.1 The Behavioural Insights Team's EAST Framework for Effective Behavioral Approaches

Make It Easy

- *Harness the power of defaults:* We have a strong tendency to go with the default or preset option, since it is easy to do so. Making an option the default makes it more likely to be adopted.
- *Reduce the "hassle factor" of taking up a service:* The effort required to perform an action often puts people off. Reducing the effort required can increase uptake or response rates.
- *Simplify messages:* Making the message clear often results in a significant increase in response rates to communications. In particular, it's useful to identify how a complex goal can be broken down into simpler, easier actions.
- *Example: Auto-enrollment into pension schemes.* In the first six months after employees in large firms were automatically enrolled into pension schemes, participation rates rose from 61 percent to 83 percent.

Make It Attractive

- *Attract attention:* We are more likely to do something that draws our attention. Ways of doing this include the use of images, color, or personalization.
- *Design rewards and sanctions for maximum effect*: Financial incentives are often highly effective, but alternative incentive designs—such as lotteries—also work well and often cost less.
- *Example: Drawing the attention of those who fail to pay road tax.* When letters to nonpayers of car tax included a picture of the offending vehicle, payment rates rose from 40 percent to 49 percent.

Make It Social

- *Show that most people perform the desired behavior:* Describing what most people do in a particular situation encourages others to do the same. Similarly, policy makers should be wary of inadvertently reinforcing a problematic behavior by emphasizing its high prevalence.
- *Use the power of networks:* We are embedded in a network of social relationships, and those we come into contact with shape our actions. Governments can foster networks to enable collective action, provide mutual support, and encourage behaviors to spread from peer to peer.
- *Encourage people to make a commitment to others:* We often use commitment devices to voluntarily "lock ourselves" into doing something in advance. The social nature of these commitments is often crucial.
- *Example: Using social norms to increase tax payments.* When people were told in letters from Her Majesty's Revenue and Customs that most people pay their tax on time, it increased payment rates significantly. The most successful message led to a 5 percent increase in payments.

box continues next page

Box 6.1 The Behavioural Insights Team's EAST Framework for Effective Behavioral Approaches *(continued)*

Make It Timely

- *Make it timely:* Prompt people when they are likely to be most receptive. The same offer made at different times can have drastically different levels of success. Behavior is generally easier to change when habits are already disrupted, such as around major life events.
- *Consider the immediate costs and benefits:* We are more influenced by costs and benefits that take effect immediately than those delivered later. Policy makers should consider whether the immediate costs or benefits can be adjusted (even slightly), given that they are so influential.
- *Help people plan their response to events:* There is a substantial gap between intentions and actual behavior. A proven solution is to prompt people to identify the barriers to action, and develop a specific plan to address them.
- *Example: Increasing payment rates through text messages.* Prompting those owing Courts Service fines with a text message 10 days before the bailiffs are to be sent to a person's home doubles the value of payments made, without the need for further intervention.

Source: Service et al. 2014.

---

received a worksheet with their water bill. The sheet included various steps that residents could take to cut back how much water they were using. Options included washing their cars less frequently and watering their gardens more efficiently.

Independent of the type of project, the pilot intervention teams stressed the importance of engaging the counterpart when determining the precise details of any intervention. This provides the vital input of local practitioners. In the case of Costa Rica, the final pilot needed the water authority's local insights to avoid ineffectual messages and to ensure that the intervention was culturally relevant.

Step 3: Define Pilot Size and Scope

The literature on conducting RCTs offers extensive details on how to carry out a pilot that is representative, scientifically valid (that is, with enough statistical power), and practically useful. This will necessarily require forethought about the appropriate sample size and selection criteria (age, sex, income, education, social class, and so on). Every effort should be made to eliminate opportunities for selection bias. Inclusion should be determined as much as possible by the proximity of a group or individual to the policy problem in question. It is advisable to make the inclusion criteria restrictive enough to narrow the sample to one that is clearly defined, while being broad enough to generalize to the population of interest.

On occasion, the pilot size may turn out to be self-selective. This proved the case in the Costa Rica pilot, where the problem at hand concerned a bounded geographical area. The neighborhood of Belén comprises a population of 21,633 inhabitants in 6,011 individual dwellings. In contrast, the problem of low tax receipts encountered by the Guatemalan tax authorities is national in scope. To ensure the sample was representative, only taxpayers who had failed to pay or were late in paying were selected. The sample included 31,000 participants randomly selected from the country's four main regions: North, West, South, and Central. As for scope, the trial was limited to the payment of income tax.

The problems associated with early childhood development, as targeted by the case study of a Nicaraguan conditional cash transfer program (Atención a Crisis), are nationally relevant as well. However, in this particular instance, the national government asked the pilot coordinators to focus on municipalities in the north of the country, where other trials of early childhood development interventions were already in progress. As a consequence, the RCTs took place in around 100 rural communities in this region. The selected communities spanned three municipalities.

Required Skills and Associated Challenges during Project Design and Implementation

The generic skills necessary for designing and implementing a project of any kind—be it behavior-led or not—are clearly required at this stage. The tasks range from undertaking a needs assessment evaluation or project goal appraisal to mapping out a budgeting plan or partnership agreement.

Research Method Expertise

More specifically, the team must include an individual with experience in designing and rolling out RCTs. Several intervention team members cited the value of having an econometrician on board to ensure that the sample size and other features of the RCT were statistically valid and meaningful.

Expertise in qualitative research and statistical analysis in general is also highly valuable. The BIT includes specialists in social psychology and economic psychology as well. For the Guatemala pilot, the project coordinator worked closely with the BIT's head of research and head of international development. The partnership also included the support of one of the team's research analysts.

Balanced Skills for Multifunctional Teams

In general, it is important to balance team members from an academic background with those with a "hands-on" knowledge of how policy making and government work in practice. All of the initial pilots benefited from civil servants or other practitioner-level staff who could advise on how organizational systems operated and how practically feasible the proposed interventions might be.

Levels of computerization and data automatization, for example, are far more limited in LMICs than in most high-income country contexts. In Costa Rica, the World Bank team spent two full days with members of the billing department to understand how the suggested customer prompts might be integrated into the water authority's existing systems. Attaching physical stickers to the water bills, although labor-intensive, was discovered to be more realistic than trying to integrate individualized messaging into the printed bills of separate control groups.

In Guatemala, a cross-functional team within the Tax Authority was established to coordinate the trial because of poor communication among the authority's key decision makers. The team consisted of around 30 people from a range of technical, managerial, and policy positions. From this group, two working groups were set up to oversee the letter and website-based trials. The team also had the assistance of around 10 support staff.

The experience of the Nicaragua team was slightly different from the others because of the lack of capacity and knowledge within the counterpart's organization. This led the pilot coordinators to contract technical experts from external agencies including a software company, a local telecommunications operator, and an educational nonprofit. The core team comprised around half a dozen people, made up largely of economists with RCT experience and analysts knowledgeable about behavioral approaches and early childhood development.

Associated Challenges
Improving Data Collection

Relevant data are often limited or not available, which presents challenges when determining a project's design. In some circumstances, it may be necessary to accept that the quantity of variables and frequency of data will be lower than a comparable study in a better-resourced LMIC context.

In cases where information does not exist, it could also be appropriate to establish systems to improve data collection and analysis. In the case of the Guatemalan Tax Authority, for instance, the project's coordinators helped create a unique dataset. The process of establishing Excel worksheets and Access documents took around four months to complete. Improving communication between different institutions or government agencies may also prove a lucrative means of addressing data gaps, which in turn benefits their day-to-day operations. To that end, a working group of data managers from across the Tax Authority was set up as part of the Guatemala pilot. The idea was to collate existing data, not generate new information. This coordinated approach increased the pilot project's likelihood of success while also leading to improvements in data collection and communication between systems that promise other long-term benefits for the counterpart.

It may be that *access* to information, rather than availability per se, represents a more prominent challenge for project managers. In such circumstances, the example of the Costa Rica pilot is potentially instructive. The program coordinator requested that the participating mayor write an endorsement letter for the pilot participants, facilitating access to relevant information across different ministries and government agencies. This opened doors across government as well as giving impetus and credibility to the pilot.

Behavioral Insights for Development • http://dx.doi.org/10.1596/978-1-4648-1120-3

Increasing Implementation Speed

As with any innovative policy intervention, complications and delays in the implementation phase are not uncommon. The period between designing and implementing a behavior-oriented trial program varies from anywhere between two months to one year. Factors that drive the time frame are the commitment of the counterpart and their participation; data access and viability; budgetary support; size of the pilot team; and the involvement of key decision makers and influencers.

The depth and thoroughness of initial research and hypothesis building has a strong influence on project timelines as well. Testing intervention ideas with focus groups, for example, will inevitably extend the lead up to implementation. Owing to the extensive case-based literature on behavior theory and tax, the Guatemalan RCT was able to proceed to implementation without a lengthy analysis period. That said, the project coordinator chose not to invest time calculating a probable target increase in tax return, determining that such a process would cause delays in implementation and provide little practical benefit.

The comparatively fast pace of implementation was also influenced by the "test, learn, adapt" approach, which allows for corrections and modifications to be made dynamically once the trial has started. The approach is similar in principle to the idea of "minimum viable products" used in fast-growth consumer markets, whereby rudimentary prototypes are quickly manufactured, tested, and redesigned accordingly.

Bureaucratic delays can further dog the initiation of pilot programs. Project coordinators would do well to consider earmarking internal resources to deal with administrative tasks, especially during the project marketing and approval stages. Internal knowledge of the counterpart's decision-making and other organizational processes can be highly beneficial in this regard.

Establishing local contact points can prove vital in speeding up the implementation process as well. This involves identifying key personnel and building up personal relationships with them as soon as possible. Such networking helps avoid time-consuming obstacles and misunderstandings in the preparatory stages as well as during the trial period itself. With the Guatemala pilot, for instance, last-minute alterations were required in the trial process because the team could not determine the availability of a color printer within the Tax Authority office. In light of the individuals' importance to a project's success, project coordinators should be alert to conditions conducive to working with key personnel and seek to avoid delaying the pilots so long that those people move on or momentum is lost. The same risk is true concerning policy environments, which can also change quickly.

As a final point regarding implementation speed, it is often necessary to fit RCTs within specific time periods or to tie them to specific events. In the Guatemala case, for instance, it was imperative that the project be rolled out during the months just preceding the end of the tax year given the critical nature of this period for the declaration and payment of taxes. Consideration of optimal calendar dates for RCTs should thus be considered as a priority for project implementation.

Analyzing the Results

The Nicaragua pilot concerning the impacts of conditional cash transfers on child development ran for one year (fall 2014 to fall 2015), after which a full analysis of the results was undertaken. An assessment was carried out to determine the physical outcomes for the children of participating parents, such as in their basic health, nutrition, and motor skills. This initial analysis phase also included other standardized testing for cognitive and noncognitive development.

Feedback loops built into the RCT is another monitoring mechanism to evaluate early impacts. Every week, participants in the Nicaragua pilot were invited to participate in a quiz. Parents were asked a trivia question related to the childhood development information they had received via SMS. Those answering correctly entered a lottery to win credit for their mobile phones. For the program coordinators, meanwhile, the quiz responses provided a valuable snapshot of how the trial was progressing. The ability of the project coordinators to gather near real-time feedback differs dramatically from most interventions by the Bank, where policy impacts and their consequent analysis fit to a long-term, post hoc timeline. This speed of feedback also proved popular with the counterpart, which could not only get a feel for the pilot's initial impact but could also consider how SMS technology might be used for interventions in other policy areas as well.

Simplicity emerged as a core factor in the success of the various case studies. In Guatemala, for example, efforts were made to make only the slightest modifications to the various letters sent to errant taxpayers. This had the benefit of ensuring that the recipient was in no doubt as to the message being communicated. Furthermore, it reduced the externalities at the analysis stage, enabling the project coordinators to home in on the individual messages and make a statistically accurate assessment of their comparable effectiveness. Yet another advantage of making only small, simple modifications was that it required little or no additional cost. The Guatemalan Tax Authority did not have to invest in additional resources or extra manpower with the letter-based pilot. It was already sending out the letters, so changing a line or two made no material difference to the logistical or administrative process.

The Importance of Partnerships

In all the pilot projects, the Bank partnered with relevant local government agencies. In the case of the Guatemala and Costa Rica pilots, internal teams were set up by the Tax Authority and the water utility, respectively, to lead the pilot's implementation. In the case of Nicaragua, lack of resources meant the Bank had to implement the RCT itself without operational assistance from the Ministry of the Family (MIFAMILIA). Instead, it contracted assistance from external partners, including a telecom company (which provided hardware), a software developer (which designed the programming and implemented the SMS delivery service), a research firm (which undertook data collection and other quantitative and qualitative research tasks), and an educational nonprofit (which advised on the project design). Overall, the various trial teams in Nicaragua numbered around 20–30 people on average, plus additional support staff.

The Nicaragua pilot relied on in-house expertise in behavioral theory, with some additional support from its nonprofit partner and relevant case study material in the literature. The Guatemala pilot, in contrast, received considerable support from the U.K.-based BIT, including field-based advice and implementation assistance. The project coordinator in Costa Rica also contracted advisory support from an external behavioral expert, the U.S.-based think tank ideas42. This partnership focused primarily on the project's design stage and did not involve support from ideas42 in the field.

Partnerships with expert third parties can make a valuable contribution to the pilot process. The main value that behavior experts such as the BIT and ideas42 bring to the table is the practical experience from undertaking similar trials in other geographies. On the downside, contracting external advisers inevitably increases the overall cost of an RCT. Bureaucratic and contractual delays associated with establishing the partnership may also occur.

The ideal scenario is for the counterpart to provide as much in-house capacity as possible. That most behavioral interventions rest on modifying standard systems should mean that existing resources will largely suffice when implementing an RCT. It may be necessary to provide some training of counterpart staff or assist with developing external advisory support to advise domestic institutions on BE-based interventions.

General Lessons Learned

The Benefits of Simplicity

One key learning across all the pilot projects was the importance of simplicity in both the project's design and implementation. The principle of simplicity applies as much to the project's purpose (what key behavioral change is desired?) as to the project's design (what key nudge[s] will be used?) and the participants' role (what key shift in behavior is required from the target population?). The latter point is of particular importance. As a broad rule for all BE interventions, the more complicated the presentation of the request is to individuals or the more labor-intensive its completion, the less likely people are to change their habits and follow the desired prompt.

An added benefit of this approach is seen at the analysis stage. Simplicity helps reduce potential externalities, thus enabling the project coordinators to home in on the individual messages and make a statistically accurate assessment of their comparable effectiveness. Cost advantages may also emerge. For example, the simplicity of the worksheet sent with the water bill to the residents of Belén required far fewer resources than would have been needed to customize the bill for each client.

The Need for Flexibility

The experimental nature of BE theory, coupled with its relatively nascent application to the policy space, puts a primacy on the ability to be flexible and ready to adapt. Because behavior-related interventions are so intimately tied up in respondents' reactions to external "nudge" factors, and because these reactions are neither homogenous nor entirely predictable, BE projects tend to be extremely dynamic.

The need for flexibility is further accentuated by the interconnected nature of project delivery. Unlike with some policy mechanisms, BE projects cannot be run in isolation. This is true even at a comparatively small pilot level. Projects need to be integrated into existing policy delivery structures, thus requiring high levels of participation, often across multiple departments. This internal requirement may introduce competing priorities or agendas, thereby increasing the need for project coordinators to demonstrate versatility.

The Importance of Replicability

Remaining mindful of the above proviso about flexibility, an important consideration guiding the pilot coordinators was the ability to potentially replicate the pilot interventions elsewhere, particularly in other LMIC settings. This motive reemphasized the preference for simple interventions that did not require elaborate technology or highly specific expertise to implement.

The Costa Rica pilot is illustrative in this respect. Had the project implementer been a highly resourced country such as the United States or a utility company in another high-income country, it might have been feasible to personalize bills to contain messages related directly to the recipient's relative consumption. Most LMIC municipalities and utilities, however, lack the necessary technological capacity for such an endeavor, as was the case in Belén. Hence, the project coordinators resolved to structure its intervention around generic colored stickers. The office in charge of stuffing bills into envelopes received access to a spreadsheet that told staff which sticker or postcard to use with each bill upon entering the meter number of a household in the experimental sample. The intervention may be low-tech, but its replication potential is far higher than a more complex system would be.

Conclusions

Central America proved to be a fertile ground for applying behavioral insights into public policy. Despite a need to raise awareness of the potential usefulness of the behavioral approach, we were surprised, if anything, by our counterparts' enthusiastic adoption of these ideas. Once we introduced the concepts, and especially examples of applications elsewhere, we found that there was much latent demand for this type of development solution from our counterparts. It was the resource constraints of the Bank teams that limited the activities that we undertook and which we report in this book to a manageable number.

Behavioral Insights for Development • http://dx.doi.org/10.1596/978-1-4648-1120-3

Our interventions also show the different scale at which behavioral insights can be applied in policy, from the local level to nationwide interventions. Our examples span a tax authority, a multisectoral program focused on early childhood education, and a municipality. In all these settings we found great receptiveness to the focus on concrete problems.

Similarly, our counterparts quickly embraced the idea of exploring practical solutions that make use of existing systems. Not requiring a dedicated data collection effort was important for the adoption of behavioral approaches, because authorities in all contexts emphasized the limited resources available to them. We turned the limited resources and capacity from a constraint to an opportunity to explore together with our counterparts creative solutions that otherwise may not have been tried. Our interventions show that applying behavioral insights into public policies is not just for rich countries. In fact, it may well be particularly suited and attractive for many development contexts.

Since we started these pilot interventions there has been much progress in the application of behavioral insights. Since then, in the context of development, the World Bank's publication of *World Development Report 2015: Mind, Society, and Behavior* (World Bank 2015) and recent creation of the Mind, Behavior, and Development (eMBeD) Unit have provided a foundation, both intellectually and operationally. Established players in this space have grown, and many new ones have been established. Countries across the globe are setting up dedicated behavioral insights teams, sometimes modeled after the original BIT in the United Kingdom but often innovating in the process. Many new trials are proving that interventions can often be scaled up. The ground has never been more fertile for applying behavioral insights for development.

Notes

1. The BIT, ideas42, and U.S. Internal Revenue Service all provide an extensive array of examples of behaviorally informed tax-related programs.
2. For more information on these two systems, see Kahneman (2011).

References

BIT (Behavioural Insights Team). 2012. "Applying Behavioral Insights to Reduce Fraud, Error and Debt." Research summary and trial reports, BIT, Cabinet Office, London.

Kahneman, Daniel. 2011. *Thinking, Fast and Slow*. New York: Farrar, Straus, and Giroux.

Service, Owain, Michael Hallsworth, David Halpern, Felicity Algate, Rory Gallagher, Sam Nguyen, Simon Ruda, and Michael Sanders. 2014. "EAST: Four Simple Ways to Apply Behavioral Insights." Behavioral insights framework guide, Behavioural Insights Team, Cabinet Office, London.

Thaler, Richard H., and Cass R. Sunstein. 2008. *Nudge: Improving Decisions about Health, Wealth, and Happiness*. New Haven, CT: Yale University Press.

World Bank. 2015. *World Development Report 2015: Mind, Society, and Behavior*. Washington, DC: World Bank.

Environmental Benefits Statement

The World Bank Group is committed to reducing its environmental footprint. In support of this commitment, we leverage electronic publishing options and print-on-demand technology, which is located in regional hubs worldwide. Together, these initiatives enable print runs to be lowered and shipping distances decreased, resulting in reduced paper consumption, chemical use, greenhouse gas emissions, and waste.

We follow the recommended standards for paper use set by the Green Press Initiative. The majority of our books are printed on Forest Stewardship Council (FSC)–certified paper, with nearly all containing 50–100 percent recycled content. The recycled fiber in our book paper is either unbleached or bleached using totally chlorine-free (TCF), processed chlorine-free (PCF), or enhanced elemental chlorine-free (EECF) processes.

More information about the Bank's environmental philosophy can be found at http://www.worldbank.org/corporateresponsibility.